Karen Brown's
FRANCE
Charming Bed & Breakfasts

Written by
CLARE BROWN

Illustrations by Barbara Tapp
Cover Painting by Jann Pollard

Karen Brown's Country Inn Series

Karen Brown Titles

Dedicated with boundless love
to

Heidi and Bill
Karen and Rick
Kim and Christian

The painting on the front cover is a scene in Provence

Editors: Karen Brown, June Brown, Clare Brown, Kim Brown Holmsen, Iris Sandilands, Gretchen DeAndre.

Illustrations: Barbara Tapp; Cover painting: Jann Pollard.

Maps: Susanne Lau Alloway—Greenleaf Design & Graphics; Back cover photo: William H. Brown.

Copyright © 1989, 1992, 1993, 1995, 1997, 1998 by Karen Brown's Guides.

This book or parts thereof may not be reproduced in any form without obtaining written permission from the publisher: Karen Brown's Guides, P.O. Box 70, San Mateo, CA 94401, USA, email: karen@karenbrown.com.

Distributed by Fodor's Travel Publications, Inc., 201 East 50th Street, New York, NY 10022, USA.

Distributed in the United Kingdom by Random House UK, 20 Vauxhall Bridge Road, London, SW1V 2SA, phone: 44 171 973 9000, fax: 44 171 840 8408.

Distributed in Australia by Random House Australia, 20 Alfred Street, Milsons Point, Sydney NSW 2061, Australia, phone: 61 2 9954 9966, fax: 61 2 9954 4562.

Distributed in New Zealand by Random House New Zealand, 18 Poland Road, Glenfield, Auckland, New Zealand, phone: 64 9 444 7197, fax: 64 9 444 7524.

Distributed in South Africa by Random House South Africa, Endulani, East Wing, 5A Jubilee Road, Parktown 2193, South Africa, phone: 27 11 484 3538, fax: 27 11 484 6180.

A catalog record for this book is available from the British Library.

Library of Congress Cataloging-in-Publication Data

Brown, Clare.
  Karen Brown's France : charming bed & breakfasts / written by
Clare Brown ; illustrations by Barbara Tapp ; cover painting by Jann
Pollard. -- Totally rev. 6th ed.
    p. cm. -- (Karen Brown's country inn series)
    Includes index.
    ISBN 0-930328-68-X (pb)
    1. Bed and breakfast accommodations--France--Guidebooks.
2. France—Guidebooks. I. Brown, Karen, 1956- . II. Title.
III. Series.
  TX907.5.F7B75 1997a
  647.9444'03--dc21   97-11558
                                                              CIP

Contents

Introduction

Travelers with a sense of adventure can truly experience France and get to know the French by journeying beyond Paris and exploring the countryside. The way of life outside Paris ("in the provinces," as the French say) is a fascinating reflection of French history and culture—the impact of modern civilization is felt, but a pronounced respect for tradition and quality of life remains. Beyond Paris, the land is like a treasure chest: royal forests with graceful deer, romantic castles casting their images onto serene lakes, picturesque villages with half-timbered houses, vineyards edged with roses, meadows of fragrant lavender, fields of vibrant yellow sunflowers, medieval walled cities perched upon mountain tops, and wild coastlines—all waiting to be discovered.

ABOUT BED & BREAKFAST TRAVEL

The bed and breakfast formula is for any traveler who wants to experience the **real** France, its people and culture. There is a social aspect to this style of travel that is not found in the normal tourist experience. You have ample opportunities to meet and exchange ideas with other travelers (usually Europeans) as well as to get to know your hosts and their families, many times making lasting friendships. Single travelers will love the friendliness of bed and breakfast stays because they will not feel alone. Bed and breakfast travel is also tailor made for families with children—the informality, convenience, and reasonable rates make travel a pleasure. Note: Many places also offer family accommodation with several bedrooms and a small kitchen.

ACCOMMODATIONS—WHAT TO EXPECT

Bed and breakfast accommodation, in most cases, means a bedroom rented in the private home of a French family. Throughout this guide, the French term *chez* used before a family name translates as "at the home of" and is an accurate phrase when describing the type of accommodation and ambiance that you can expect. However, do not feel that to travel the bed and breakfast route means you will be roughing it. Although some of the least expensive choices in our guide offer very simple rooms, it is possible to choose places to stay that offer sumptuous accommodations—as beautiful as you will find in the most luxurious hotels, at a fraction of the cost. So, this book is definitely not just for the budget-conscious traveler, but for anyone who wants to meet the French people and experience their exceptional hospitality.

The dividing line between a bed and breakfast and a "regular" hotel is sometimes very obscure. In essence, hotels are larger and offer more commercial amenities than a bed and breakfast—hotels usually have a reception desk, a staff member always on the premises, a public restaurant, telephones in the rooms, and a porter for luggage. However, nothing is truly black and white. Some of the bed and breakfasts featured in tnis guide are very sophisticated and offer every imaginable nicety including exquisite linens, fluffy bathrobes, towel warmers, hairdryers, and an assortment of the finest toiletries. As a rule of thumb, you will find that the bed and breakfast accommodations are far less expensive than a comparable room in a hotel, offer a more personalized warmth of welcome, and provide a better opportunity to meet other guests. Note: We have intentionally included a few simple, well-priced, small hotels with charm that are located in areas where we could not find a suitable bed and breakfast to offer you.

Hosts cover the entire spectrum of French society, from titled counts and countesses to country farmers. All who are listed in this guide are hospitable and have a true desire to meet and interact with their guests. It takes a special kind of person to open his home to strangers, and the French who do so are genuinely warm and friendly.

Bed and breakfasts are called *chambres d'hôtes* (literally, "guest bedrooms") and are most frequently situated in rural settings. This guide offers lodging selections in or near major tourist sites as well as in unspoiled, less-visited regions. Most hosts prefer that their bed and breakfast guests take the time to unwind by staying at least three nights (Americans have a reputation for always being in a hurry). Frequently discounts are offered for stays of a week or longer, but the advantages of longer stays in one place are far greater than just financial: it is great fun to become friends with the owners and other guests, to just *settle in*—no packing and unpacking every night. Frequently a house-party atmosphere prevails as you gather with other guests in the evening to share your travel adventures. We strongly urge you to choose one place to stay and make it your hub, going off in a different direction each day to explore the countryside. Spend time in a medieval stone-walled château evoking dreams of knights and their ladies or experience the sights and sounds of a simple farm surrounded by bucolic pasture lands. Careful reading of the descriptions in this guide will assure that the homes you select are in line with the type of welcome and accommodation you prefer. Each home is, of course, unique, offering its own special charm, yet all share one wonderful common denominator: the welcoming feeling of being treated as a cherished guest in a friend's home. We unequivocally feel there is no finer way to travel in France.

We personally visited hundreds of bed and breakfasts, traveling to remote villages and hamlets throughout France to find the finest places to stay. Even after honing down our list by prior research, we usually included only about one out of every three places seen. We made our personal selection based on individual charm, antique ambiance, romantic feel, and above all, on warmth of welcome. We chose each place to stay on its merit alone. We selected in each region the most outstanding accommodations in various price ranges. Our choices are very subjective: we have hand-picked for you those places that we like the most and think you will also enjoy.

CHAMBRES D'HÔTES & GÎTES DE FRANCE

Over 5,600 bed and breakfasts in France belong to a national organization, Gîtes de France. Members of this organization usually display the green-and-yellow Gîtes de France logo shown. Chambres d'hôtes that are members of Gîtes de France have passed an in-depth inspection by the organization and conform to a high standard of welcome and comfort. We have worked very closely with this organization to select the finest places to stay from an overwhelming list of possibilities. The majority of chambres

d'hôtes featured in this guide are part of this association. However, we also visited and have included many outstanding places that have chosen not to belong to the Gîtes de France. In the bed and breakfast description section we have put "Gîtes de France" by the name of all the properties that belong to this affiliation. The head office is: Gîtes de France, 59 Rue Saint-Lazare, 75009 Paris, France, Tel: 01.49.70.75.75, Fax: 01.42.81.28.53.

CREDIT CARDS

A few bed and breakfasts accept credit cards. When they do, we have indicated this in the description of the bed and breakfast using the following codes: AX–American Express, MC–MasterCard, VS–Visa, or simply, all major.

DRIVING & DIRECTIONS

It is important to understand some basic directions in French when locating bed and breakfasts. Signs directing to chambres d'hôtes are often accompanied by either *1ère à droite* (first road on the right) or *1ère à gauche* (first road on the left). Chambres d'Hôtes signs can vary from region to region, but most have adopted the national green-and-yellow sign of the Gîtes de France as shown on page 4.

Maps label the roads with their proper numbers, but you will find when driving that signs usually indicate a direction instead of a road number. For example, instead of finding a sign for N909 north, you will see a sign for Lyon, so you must figure out by referring to your map whether Lyon is north of where you are and if N909 leads there. The city that is signposted is often a major city quite a distance away. This may seem awkward at first, but is actually an easy system once you get your bearings.

Most bed and breakfast homes and farmhouses are located outside the town or village under which they are listed. To make finding your destination easier, specific driving instructions are given in each bed and breakfast description. However, if you become lost while looking for your lodging, find the nearest post office or public phone box (usually in the central town square or in front of the post office) and call your hosts for directions. It is a good idea to keep a French telephone credit card handy for phone calls. In a pinch, bars and petrol stations will usually allow you to use their phones (they will charge you after the call). An added suggestion: Always plan to arrive at your destination before nightfall—road signs are difficult to see after dark.

LANGUAGE—LEVEL OF ENGLISH SPOKEN

Possessing even the most rudimentary knowledge and exposure to French will make your trip a thousand times more rewarding and enjoyable. Buy a French phrase book before you leave home and do a little practicing. You can always get by: usually there is someone around who speaks at least a little English, and the French are accustomed to dealing with non-French-speaking travelers. It is helpful to carry paper and pencil to write down numbers for ease of comprehension, as well as a French phrase book and/or dictionary. If pronunciation seems to be a problem, you can then indicate the word or phrase in writing.

The level of English spoken in the bed and breakfasts in this guide runs the gamut from excellent to none at all. Because some of you would have fun practicing your high-school French while others would feel more comfortable communicating freely in English, we have indicated under each bed and breakfast description what you can expect. Levels of the host's English are indicated according to the following guidelines:

NO ENGLISH SPOKEN—a few words at best.

VERY LITTLE ENGLISH SPOKEN—a little more than the most rudimentary, or perhaps their children speak schoolroom English. More is understood than spoken.

SOME or GOOD ENGLISH SPOKEN—basic communication is possible, but longer, involved conversations are not. Speak slowly and clearly. Remember, they may understand more than they can articulate.

VERY GOOD ENGLISH SPOKEN—easy conversational English. More understood than able to express verbally.

FLUENT ENGLISH SPOKEN—can understand and communicate with ease—frequently the person has lived in Britain or the United States.

MAPS

In the back of this guide (on pages 195–206) there are 11 maps pinpointing the location of each bed and breakfast. The pertinent map number is given at the right on the *top line* of each hotel's description. To make it easier for you, we have divided each location map into a grid of four parts, a, b, c, and d, as indicated on each map's key. However, these are not detailed enough to use as road maps. Places in the countryside are very tricky to find so it is vital that you supplement our maps with more detailed ones. Some of the best are those made by Michelin who publishes two sets of regional maps—we recommend and cross-reference the series numbered from 230 to 245. So that you will know what to purchase, we have put the corresponding Michelin map number at the bottom of each lodging description. Every bed and breakfast featured in this guide can be found on these maps. (Another bonus with the Michelin maps is that historical monuments are indicated and scenic routes are highlighted in green.) Nothing can surpass the accuracy and detail of the Michelin maps, but, unfortunately, they lack an index, so it is helpful to supplement the Michelin maps with Hallwag maps (distributed by Rand McNally) which cover an amazing number of small towns and also have very useful indexes. Michelin and Hallwag maps can be purchased or special-ordered from your local bookstore.

MEALS

BREAKFAST in a bed and breakfast is usually the Continental type, including a choice of coffee (black or with hot milk), tea, or hot chocolate, bread (sometimes a croissant or wheat bread for variety), butter, and jam. The evening before, hosts will customarily ask when you want breakfast and what beverage you prefer. Sometimes they will offer a choice of location such as outside in the garden or indoors in the dining area or kitchen.

TABLE D'HÔTE means that the host serves an evening meal. Of all the special features of a bed and breakfast experience, this is one of the most outstanding—if you see "Table d'hôte" offered under the bed and breakfast description, be sure to request it! You will not have a choice of menu, but you will have a delicious, home-cooked dinner (usually the ingredients are fresh from the garden) and be able to meet fellow guests. Most frequently meals are served at one large table with the hosts joining you and the other guests, but sometimes they are served at individual or shared tables. Expect at least three courses (an appetizer, a main course, and dessert), often four or five courses (with salad and cheese being served between the entree and dessert).

Prices quoted are **always** per person and sometimes include a table wine. The price depends upon how elaborate the meal is, the sophistication of the service, the number of courses, and what beverages are included. However, whether the meal is simple or gourmet, whenever you take advantage of the table d'hôte option, you will discover a real bargain and have a truly memorable experience. Note: The price for the meal might have increased before you arrive, so be sure to check the price.

When wine is included in the price of the meal, this is noted under the description. In a simple bed and breakfast, this is usually a house wine of the region—not fancy, but usually very good. Some of the deluxe places to stay often offer an aperitif before dinner, a selection of wines with the meal, and a nightcap afterwards.

There are a few places we recommend that, in addition to offering bed and breakfast accommodations, also have a restaurant. If so, this is noted in the description.

VERY IMPORTANT: When we indicate in the bed and breakfast description that table d'hôte is available, it is **always only available by prior arrangement**—and how often varies tremendously. Some bed and breakfasts offer table d'hôte every day; others serve dinner only when a minimum number of guests want to dine or on certain nights of the week. A few hosts seem to cook only when the whim strikes them. So, in other words— always take advantage of table d'hôte when it is offered, but be sure to check with your hosts to see if the option is available then make a dinner reservation when you book your room. Also inquire what time the meal will be served. Be sure to call your host from along the way if you are running late. The French do not have large freezers stocked with frozen supplies nor microwaves to defrost a quick meal. Food is usually fresh and purchased with care the day it is prepared, making it difficult to produce an impromptu meal. If you are a late arrival and have not eaten, sometimes your host will offer a plate of cold cuts, salad, and bread, but do not expect this as it is not standard procedure. A few French terms to describe food services are listed below:

DEMI-PENSION includes breakfast and dinner with prices quoted per person. This usually saves you money.

PENSION COMPLÈTE includes breakfast, lunch, and dinner with prices quoted per person. This formula is rarely an option since most travelers prefer to be on their own for lunch.

FERME AUBERGE is a family-style restaurant, open to the public, on a working farm. These inns are actually controlled by the French government in so far as the products served must come mainly from the farm itself. The fare is usually simple and hearty, utilizing fresh meats and vegetables. The hosts do not generally sit down and share meals with their guests because they are often too busy serving.

PETS

If you miss your pet when on the road, bed and breakfast travel might be just your cup of tea. Even if not specifically mentioned in the write-up, chances are you will be greeted by a tail-wagging dog and often find a cat happily napping on the sofa. If you are traveling with your own pet, check to see if pets are accepted and what the charge will be when you make your reservation. The French love animals and some do allow you to bring your canine traveling companion.

RATES

In each bed and breakfast listing, 1998 summer rates are given for two persons in a double room, including tax, service, and Continental breakfast. Often rooms can accommodate up to four persons at additional charge and cribs and extra beds are usually available for children. Prices frequently go down if a stay is longer than three to five nights. Many places also offer small apartments or separate houses with cooking facilities that are ideal for families. Apartment rates do not include breakfast and are based on a week's stay (reservations are rarely accepted for periods of less than a week). When budgeting, a rule of thumb to remember is that usually the farther out in the country and away from large towns or tourist regions, the more inexpensive the accommodation will be. Beautifully furnished country homes and castles can be real bargains although they will cost more if located in one of the prime tourist centers. Rates quoted were given to us at the time of publication and are subject to change. Be sure to verify the current price when making a reservation.

RESERVATIONS—GENERAL INFORMATION

A few bed and breakfasts in this guide offer a degree of sophistication that approaches that of a deluxe hotel. But remember, the very essence of bed and breakfast accommodation is what makes it so special—these are private homes. It is not appropriate to just knock on the door and expect accommodation: prior reservations are essential. This also works to your advantage because most bed and breakfasts are tucked away in remote areas and it is frustrating to drive far out of your way, only to find everything is sold out. If you want to be footloose and not confined to a rigid schedule, phone from along the way to see if a room is available.

RESERVATIONS—DEPOSITS: Deposits are preferred if you are reserving several months ahead of your arrival date. Deposits are usually requested in French francs: this is for your own protection against fluctuating exchange rates. Drafts in French francs can be purchased at the main branch of many large banks. Credit cards are rarely accepted at bed and breakfasts, although they are sometimes accepted as a guarantee of arrival. Be aware that once you have paid your deposit, it is usually non refundable.

RESERVATIONS BY FAX: The majority of bed and breakfasts have installed fax machines. If so, this is a very efficient way to request a reservation. (You can use the reservation letter in French found on page 14.) Sending a fax is like telephoning: use the international code (011 from the United States), then the country code for France (33) followed by the fax number (dropping the initial 0). If dialing within France, dial the initial 0. Remember to give your fax number for their response. Note: In any written correspondence be sure to spell out the month since Europeans reverse the American system for dates. As an example, in France 4/9/98 means September 4, not April 9.

RESERVATIONS BY MAIL: Writing a letter is the most popular method for booking accommodations, but allow plenty of time. It is advisable to write well in advance so that you will have time to write to your second choice if your first is unavailable. Allow at least a week each way for air mail to and from France. If you do not speak French, you can make a copy and use the reservation letter supplied on page 14. Be sure to spell out the month—see note in previous paragraph.

RESERVATIONS BY TELEPHONE: If you speak French (or if we have indicated under the bed and breakfast description that fluent English is spoken by the owner), we recommend you call for a reservation. With a telephone call you can discuss what is available and most suited to your needs. It is best to always follow up with a letter and a deposit in French francs if requested. Telephone reservations are accepted by most bed and breakfast homes, but if there is a language barrier, it will be frustrating and difficult to communicate your wants. (Remember the time difference when calling: Paris is six hours ahead of New York.) To place a call, dial the international code (011 from the United States), then the country code for France (33) followed by the telephone number (dropping the initial 0). If dialing within France, dial the initial 0.

RESERVATIONS & CHECK-IN: Bed and breakfasts are not hotels—they are private homes. There is not always someone "at the front desk" to check you in, so it is courteous to call the day you are expected to reconfirm your reservation and to advise what time you anticipate arriving. If you have made arrangements to dine, ask what hour dinner will be served and be sure to be on time or you will hold up the "dinner party."

RESERVATIONS & CANCELLATIONS: If it is necessary for you to cancel your reservation for any reason, please phone (or write far in advance) to alert the proprietor. Bed and breakfasts often have only one or two rooms to rent and are thus severely impacted financially if they hold a room for a "no-show." It is embarrassing to hear stories from gracious innkeepers who have stayed up until late at night, waiting to welcome the guest who never came.

TELEPHONES

TELEPHONES—HOW TO CALL WITHIN FRANCE: It is very important to know how to make telephone calls within France. If you are running later than your expected time of arrival, stop at a public telephone to advise your hosts. There are two kinds of telephones within France—coin phones and credit-card phones. Be sure to carry with you some franc coins—these are used for most telephones. The other type of public telephone accepts only special credit cards and although at first this seems complicated, it is actually easy. Stop by a post office (*bureau de poste*) and buy a credit card for a specified amount of credit. You place this card into a slot on the telephone; then, when you complete your call, the cost is automatically subtracted from the total available credit.

TELEPHONES—HOW TO CALL THE USA: Unlike hotels, most bed and breakfasts rarely have direct-dial telephones in the guestrooms. If your hosts do not have a telephone you can use, public telephones are readily available. The best bet is to use an international telephone card—with one of these you can make a local call within France and be connected with your USA operator (ask your long-distance carrier what access number to use). The charge will appear on your telephone bill. All of the long-distance telephone companies in the United States offer this option.

TOURIST INFORMATION

Syndicat d'Initiative is the name for the tourist offices found in all towns and resorts in France. When you are on the road, it is very helpful to pop into one of these offices signposted with a large "I" (which stands for information). The agents gladly give advice on local events, timetables for local trains, buses and boats, and often have maps and brochures on the region's points of interest. They can also help with locating bed and breakfast accommodation. Before you depart for France, additional information can be obtained by writing to one of the tourist offices listed below:

French Government Tourist Office, 444 Madison Ave., 16th Floor, New York, NY 10022, USA

French Government Tourist Office, 9454 Wilshire Blvd., Suite 715, Beverly Hills, CA 90212, USA

French Government Tourist Office, 676 N. Michigan Ave., Suite 3360, Chicago, IL 60611, USA

French Government Tourist Office, 178 Piccadilly, London W1V OAL, England

French Government Tourist Office, 30 St. Patrick St., Suite 700, Toronto, Ontario, M57 3A3, Canada

The above tourist offices can be contacted only by mail. If you want to call for specific information, in the United States you can telephone 1-900-990-0040. Calls to this number will be charged to your phone bill at the rate of 50 cents per minute.

Reservation Letter

To: Bed and Breakfast, name and address

Monsieur/Madame:

Nous serons _____ personnes.
We have (number) of persons in our party

Nous voudrions réserver pour _____ nuit(s)
We would like to reserve for (number of nights)

       du _____
       from (date of arrival)

       au _____
       to (date of departure),

       une chambre à deux lits _____
       a room(s) with twin beds

       une chambre au grand lit _____
       a room(s) with double bed(s)

       une chambre avec un lit supplémentaire _____
       room(s) with an extra bed

       avec toilette et baignoire ou douche privée _____
       with private toilet and bathtub or shower

Veuilliez confirmer la réservation en nous communicant le prix de la chambre et la somme d'arrhes que vous souhaitez. Dans l'attente de votre réponse, nous vous prions d'agréer, Messieurs, Mesdames, l'expression de nos sentiments distingués.

Please advise availability, rate of room and deposit needed. We will be waiting for your confirmation and send our kindest regards.

Your name and address and fax number (if applicable)

Bed & Breakfast Descriptions

Harry Lammot Belin (who is from the United States) owns the Château Andelot, but do not worry—this is not a castle bought on a whim by a wealthy American wanting to pretend to be Lord of the Manor—the property is his family home. It was Harry's grandfather who returned to the beautiful Jura region of France many years ago with his cousin Pierre du Pont looking for their roots and purchased one of their 12th-century ancestral castles, Château Andelot, as a holiday abode. When Harry came into the picture, the castle was deteriorating. His solution was to bring the château back to its former glory and recover some of the staggering costs of renovation by opening it as a bed and breakfast. Today the guest enjoys an intimate, picture-perfect, stone fort, approached through an original 12$^\text{th}$ century gate, fortified by a pair of turreted towers. From the courtyard (and also from within the château) there are sweeping vistas of rolling forested hills. The interior is stunning: elegant antique furnishings (mostly purchased by Harry's grandfather) are enhanced by sumptuous fabrics in rich colors, all put together by a talented decorator. *Directions:* The château is about midway between Bourg en Bresse and Lons le Saunier. Exit the N83 at Saint Amour and take the D3 east towards Saint Julien. After 12 km, just before village of Andelot, the château is signposted on your left.

CHÂTEAU ANDELOT (Gîtes de France)
Host: Harry Lammot Belin
Rue de l'Eglise
39320 Andelot-Morval, France
Tel: 03.84.85.41.49, Fax: 03.84.85.46.74
www.karenbrown.com/france/chateauandelot.html
6 rooms with private bathrooms
Double: 500F–600F, Suite: from 800F
Table d'hôte: 175–225F per person
Open Apr to Nov, Fluent English spoken, Credit cards: all major
Region: Jura; Michelin Map 243

Although Les Hêtres Rouges is located in Burgundy, it was never associated with wine growing. Its ancestry was that of a hunting lodge—many forests still abound where wild boar roam. Wrought-iron gates lead into a large park and the pretty peach-colored 18th-century manor house with pretty gray-blue shutters. An old wooden staircase twists up to the bedrooms which are romantically tucked up under the eaves. Each bedroom is lovingly decorated by your charming hostess, Christiane Bugnet, with antique furniture and pretty Laura Ashley fabrics. Christiane is an artist who paints in the vibrant colors of the countryside, which she also used throughout in her decor. My favorite bedroom overlooks the back garden and is painted yellow with a pretty floral print on the bedspreads and curtains. If you are planning to use Les Hêtres Rouges as a hub to explore this glorious region of France, splurge and request the suite. Here you have your own romantic, two-story, ivy-covered cottage, adorable with pink shutters (adorned with heart-shaped cutouts), its own kitchen, and a private little garden terrace where breakfast is served. *Directions:* Located between Beaune and Dijon. From the autoroute A31, take the Nuit-Saint-Georges exit. Almost as soon as you exit the highway, follow the signs that lead back over the expressway towards Seurre. After 3 km, turn right towards Quincey. Go through Quincey and continue on for 4 km to Argilly. As you arrive in Argilly, watch for the Chambres d'Hôtes sign on the right, marking the entrance to Les Hêtres Rouges.

LES HÊTRES ROUGES (*Gîtes de France*)
Hostess: Christiane Bugnet
Antilly, 21700 Argilly, France
Tel: 03.80.62.53.98, Fax:03.80.62.54.85
www.karenbrown.com/france/leshetresrouges.html
4 rooms with private bathrooms
Double: 430F–600F
No table d'hôte
Open all year, Some English spoken
Region: Burgundy; Michelin Map 243

Although close to Avignon, you almost seem in another world approaching through the barren, rock-studded landscape to Le Rocher Pointu, a lovely old stone farmhouse softened by dark-brown shutters and huge terra-cotta pots brimming with flowers. It must have seemed an overwhelming task to make the house livable when Annie and André Malek bought it a few years ago—there was not even running water. Now, not only is there running water, there is a beautiful swimming pool (if you are somewhat prudish, be forewarned that you might find most of the guests swimming *au naturel*). The interior has been renovated maintaining the natural appeal of the original old farmhouse: white walls, massive beamed ceilings, and country antiques add to the appealing ambiance. Upstairs are four bedrooms—my favorite is the Clair de Lune room with a handsome wood French Provençal headboard and a pretty view from the casement windows. There is a kitchen and barbecue area for guests' use. *Directions:* Aramon is located about 10 km southwest of Avignon. From Avignon, follow the D2 south along the west bank of the Rhône. Turn right, in the direction of Saze, when you come to D126. After 2.3 km you will come to the sign for Le Rocher Pointu. Turn left at the sign and follow the road to the Le Rocher Pointu.

LE ROCHER POINTU (Gîtes de France)
Hosts: Annie & André Malek
Plan de Deve
30390 Aramon, France
Tel: 04.66.57.41.87, Fax: 04 66.57.01.77
E-mail: amk@imaginet.fr
www.karenbrown.com/france/lerocherpointu.html
4 rooms with private bathrooms
Double: 360F–435F, Apt: 465F–590F without breakfast
No table d'hôte
Open all year, Good English spoken
Region: Provence; Michelin Map 245

A breathtakingly lovely Renaissance castle, the Château de la Verrerie offers the comfort and refinement of an English country home coupled with incomparable French flair for artful decoration and fine cuisine. Each guest bedroom is spacious and unique, with its own color scheme and special charm. A fine example of a room is one done in shades of rose, complemented by a gray marble fireplace and fine antique furnishings. A writing desk placed near the window overlooks the well-manicured lawns and gardens which extend to nearby woods. The adjoining spacious bathroom comes complete with claw-footed tub. An inviting guest sitting room combines warmth and elegance to a perfect degree, offering plenty of comfortable seating, good lighting, and reading materials in several languages. In addition to relaxing in this esthetically beautiful setting, you can also tour the historic chapel and Renaissance gallery and enjoy gourmet lunches and dinners served in the nearby Auberge d'Helène. This restaurant, found in a cozy and atmospheric 18th-century cottage, features regional dishes and fine wines. *Directions:* Located 76 km southeast of Orléans and 44 km northeast of Bourges. From Bourges travel north on the D940 for 34 km. At La Chapelle d'Angillon travel northeast on D926 for 6 km to Le Grand Rond. La Verrerie, 4 km north, is reached by following D39 and D89.

CHÂTEAU DE LA VERRERIE
Hosts: Comte & Comtesse Béraud de Vogüé
Oizon, 18700 Aubigny-sur-Nère, France
Tel: 02.48.81.51.60, Fax: 02.48.58.21.25
www.karenbrown.com/france/chateaudelaverrerie.html
12 rooms with private bathrooms
Double: 1,000–1,420F
*Table d'hôte: 490F per person, includes wine**
**Restaurant menu: 95F–200F*
Closed Christmas, Fluent English spoken
Credit cards: all major
Region: Centre; Michelin Map 238

La Chavinière, an enchanting pale-yellow 18th-century stone manor with white shutters, is owned by the gracious Thierry Morel and his lovely wife, Yveline. When purchased, the property was in disrepair but today the renovated home is stunning—a tribute to the exquisite taste of the Morels. All the modern enhancements have been thoughtfully added without destroying any of the authentic charm and there is an ambiance throughout of refined elegance. Heirloom antiques abound, enhanced by bouquets of freshly picked flowers and rich English fabrics. On the first floor are the comfortable, homey living room, dining room, and characterful large kitchen with its original enormous fireplace. From the hall, a beautiful wood staircase circles up to the bedrooms. All are outstanding, but my very favorite is the Chambre des Oiseaux, a corner room with a magnificent antique desk, splendid armoire, and blue country-checked bedspread. The home backs onto a garden with a sheltered terrace from which garden gates open to a park with a private pond—a tranquil oasis to relax and enjoy a good book. To the side of the house is a swimming pool. *Directions:* Located 55 km northwest of Toulouse. From the A62 (Bordeaux to Toulouse), exit at Castelsarrasin towards Beaumont de Lomagne, then 10 km after Beaumont de Lomagne (D928) turn right towards Avensac for 600 meters. Turn left and the house is signposted on the left.

LA CHAVINIÈRE (Gîtes de France)
Hosts: Yveline & Thierry Morel
32120 Avensac, France
Tel: 05.62.65.03.43, Fax: 05.62.65.03.23
5 rooms with private bathrooms
Double: 510F–910F
Table d'hôte: 110F per person
Open Mar to Nov, Good English spoken
Credit cards: MC, VS
Region: Midi-Pyrénées; Michelin Map 235

At Les Ecureuils Françoise and Lionel Menoret take great pleasure in making each guest feel special. Their small, symmetrical, two-story home with a steeply pitched roof and twin chimneys is located in the pretty little village of Cheille (well known for its very old church that miraculously has a tree growing within the wall). As you enter the front hallway, on the right is an intimate parlor which guests are welcome to use. To the left is the dining room where Françoise serves delicious meals, lovingly prepared and artfully presented. A doorway off the hall leads to the one bedroom, with the shower and washbasin in a curtained-off area and a private WC located in a separate room. The bedroom is small, but impeccably clean and very sweet in tones of soft green and rose with Laura-Ashley-like wallpaper and pretty coordinating fabric used for the headboard and drapes. Lionel, whose business is tourism, is a wealth of information on what to see and do in the area. His lovely young wife, Françoise, keeps busy managing the bed and breakfast, caring for their adorable little girls, Pauline, Gaëlle, and Gladys (who will win your heart), and tending the garden where she grows fresh vegetables for the table. *Directions:* From Azay le Rideau take D17 northwest towards the Château d'Ussé. After about 5 km, turn left at Cheille. Go past the church and continue 150 meters—you will see Les Ecureuils' sign on your left.

LES ECUREUILS   (*Gîtes de France*)
Hosts: Françoise & Lionel Menoret
Cheille, 37190 Azay Le Rideau, France
Tel: 02.47.45.39.74, Fax: 02.47.48.13 39
1 room with private bathroom
Double: 280F (2-night minimum)
Table d'hôte: 100F per person, includes wine
Open all year, Fluent English spoken
Region: Loire Valley; Michelin Map 232

La Bihourderie, a characterful long, low farmhouse draped in ivy, has a fairy-tale quality. White shuttered windows peek out from this picturesque one-story home, further enhanced by a very steep roof which is prettily accented by gabled windows. La Bihourderie is extremely appealing, and makes a well-priced base for visiting the fabulous châteaux of the Loire Valley. The tidy front courtyard of this working farm abounds with beautifully tended, colorful flower gardens. There is a separate section of the house with a private parlor just for the guests, off which you find the four bedrooms, named after works of art by Van Gogh. My favorite, Les Iris, is attractively decorated with fabrics blending with the framed copy of Van Gogh's painting of the iris. Although the farmhouse is very old, the decor is a bit bland, without an antique ambiance. However, everything is exceptionally well kept and immaculately clean. Mignès Bouin is not only a gracious hostess, but also an excellent housekeeper. When the days are warm, both breakfast and dinner (prepared from fresh produce from the farm) are served at tables set outside on the lawn behind the house, so wonderfully close to the fields that wheat almost tickles your nose. *Directions:* From Tours, take the N143 towards Loches. Go through Cormery, then turn left 10 km after Cormery in the direction of Azay-sur-Indre. The Chambres d'Hôtes sign is on your left.

LA BIHOURDERIE (Gîtes de France)
Hosts: Mignès & Christophe Bouin
37310 Azay-sur-Indre, France
Tel: 02.47.92.58.58, Fax: 02.47.92.22.19
www.karenbrown.com/france/labihourderie.html
4 rooms with private bathrooms
Double: 240F–310F
Table d'hôte: 85F per person, includes wine
Open all year, Good English spoken
Region: Loire Valley; Michelin Map 238

Arlette Vachet's English-style country cottage is at the top of our list for romantic and atmospheric bed and breakfast accommodation. Arlette is a painter and former antique dealer who has filled her cozy, ivy-covered house with a potpourri of country antiques and used her artistic talents to decorate the interior to charming perfection. Her salon is a virtual treasure trove of paintings, old furniture and objets d'art, set off by low, beamed ceilings and an old stone hearth. A comfortable couch and a crackling fire are the perfect accompaniments to an evening's aperitif before sampling one of the region's many restaurants, renowned for their fine wines and gourmet cuisine. French doors open from the garden to the ground-floor bedroom, prettily decorated in a butterfly motif in tones of forest green and pink. In addition to the first-floor room, there are two bedrooms upstairs—one small and intimate with a low, sloping ceiling covered by beautiful flowered wallpaper, the other a small suite. In addition, across the garden is a most engaging cottage for guests who want to stay a week. *Directions:* Baudrières is located 19 km southeast of Châlon-sur-Saône. From the A6 (Paris to Lyon) take the Châlon South exit. Follow the green bis Lyon signs. Go through Epervans and Ouroux-sur-Saône on D 978, then turn right on D 933 towards Simandre. After 2 km turn left at Nassey to Baudrières. La Chaumière is located across from the church.

LA CHAUMIÈRE (Gîtes de France)
Hostess: Arlette Vachet
Baudrières
71370 Saint Germain du Plain, France
Tel: 03.85.47.32.18, Fax: 03.85.47.41.42
www.karenbrown.com/france/lachaumiere.html
2 rooms, 1 suite, with private bathrooms
Double: 320F Suite: 450F
No table d'hôte
Open all year, Good English spoken
Region: Burgundy; Michelin Map 243

Ludovic and Eliane Cornillon have struck the perfect balance between rustic ambiance and luxurious comfort in their charming farmhouse found in the countryside of northern Provence. The entire farm complex dates from 1769 and is rectangular in shape, forming a tranquil central garden sheltered by weathered stone walls. A low doorway leads into the historic entry salon which has a large old hearth decorated with dried flower bouquets and interesting antique furniture including a *petain*, a piece somewhat like a large chest used for both storing flour and kneading bread dough. The adjoining dining room, formerly the stables, still displays a stone feeding trough and a little stairway leading to the attic where the hay was stored. Eliane's fresh style of cuisine features regional herbs and is complemented well by Domaine de Saint Luc wines, as Ludovic is a talented wine maker. After dinner, a good night's rest is assured in charming bedrooms, all with spotless private baths. *Directions:* La Baume de Transit is located about 24 km north of Orange. Take auto route A7 and exit at Bollène, following directions for Suze la Rousse on D94. Leave Suze la Rousse on D59 towards Saint Paul Trois Châteaux, but turn off almost immediately onto the small country road CD117 towards La Baume de Transit. Look for signs for Domaine de Saint Luc.

DOMAINE DE SAINT LUC (*Gîtes de France*)
Hosts: Eliane & Ludovic Cornillon
Le Gas du Rossignol, La Baume de Transit
26130 Saint Paul-Trois Châteaux, France
Tel: 04.75.98.11.51, Fax: 04.75.98.19.22
www.karenbrown.com/france/domainedesaintluc.html
5 rooms with private bathrooms
Double: 350F–550F
Table d'hôte: 135F per person
Closed Dec, Good English spoken by Eliane
Region: Provence; Michelin Map 245

The Château d'Arbieu is filled with family antiques, paintings, and objets d'art, yet also manages to convey a comfortable, lived-in feeling. Comte and Comtesse de Chenerilles are a young, friendly, unpretentious couple who happily welcome guests to their historic family home. Delicious, thoughtfully prepared table d'hôte dinners are enjoyed with the de Chenerilles in their pleasant dining room. Furnishings are a mix of contemporary and antique pieces accented by home-like touches such as large color photos of their children above the mantelpiece. The bedrooms are found upstairs, affording lovely views of the countryside. All the guestrooms contain beautiful antique furnishings and are decorated with tasteful, period-style wallpapers, fabrics, and artwork. Fresh flower arrangements and in-room phones add extra touches of luxury. Extensive grounds include a refreshing swimming pool and convenient pool-house kitchenette for guests' use. *Directions:* Bazas is located 60 km southeast of Bordeaux. Take autoroute A62 in the direction of Agen and Toulouse. Exit at Langon and follow signs to Bazas via D932. From Bazas, take D655 towards Casteljoux and less than 1 km outside town, look for a Chambres d'Hôtes sign that marks the long driveway to the Château d'Arbieu.

CHÂTEAU D'ARBIEU (Gîtes de France)
Hosts: Comte & Comtesse Ph. de Chènerilles
Arbieu
33430 Bazas, France
Tel: 05.56.25.11.18, Fax: 05.56.25.90.52
4 rooms, 1 suite, with private bathrooms
Double: 420F–475F
Table d'hôte: 160F per person
Closed Feb, Some English spoken
Region: Aquitaine; Michelin Map 234

For 20 years Jill and Joe Webb owned a restaurant and a hotel in Portsmouth, England, but today their talents are concentrated on a fairy-tale castle they bought in France. It has been a tremendous task to renovate the property—you have to admire their determination as they have done most of the work themselves. It is an ongoing project—the latest improvement under way (which should soon be finished) is a swimming pool. The castle is massive, so it is not surprising that the bedrooms are exceptionally large. An added bonus is that each has a wood-burning fireplace which warms the room on chilly evenings and also casement windows opening onto a view of the tranquil property. Château d'Arnac has 22 acres of woodland with a stream running through it and a small lake. What is especially fun is that this is a proper farm with sheep, pigs, chickens, and geese. Jill is an excellent cook and, in addition to wonderful dinners (using produce from their farm), serves a true English breakfast with bacon and eggs. Meals are served family-style around one large table where guests quickly become friends. Jill and Joe are charming and dedicated to ensuring that guests have a memorable stay. *Directions:* From Brive, take D38 towards Beaulieu-sur-Dordogne. When D38 meets D940, turn right towards Beaulieu. Go just about 300 meters and turn left (opposite a cemetery that is difficult to see) into the lane to the Château d'Arnac.

CHÂTEAU D'ARNAC
Hosts: Jill & Joe Webb
19120 Beaulieu-sur-Dordogne, France
5 rooms with private bathrooms
Double: 540F
Tel: 05.55.91.54.13, Fax: 05.55.91.52.62
www.karenbrown.com/france/chateaudarnac.html
Table d'hôte: 200F per person, includes wine
Open all year, Fluent English spoken
Credit cards: VS, MC
Region: Dordogne; Michelin Map 235

In the hills near Toulon, the Zerbibs opened their lovely home as a bed and breakfast. Marceau Zerbib, a talented architect, completely renovated the house so that there are now four attractive guest bedrooms, tastefully appointed in a quiet, elegant manner with country antiques enhanced by lovely fabrics. The home (a traditional Provençal-style structure with a heavy tiled roof and green shutters) has a parklike setting that is captivating. The gardens are spectacular, with a lush lawn sweeping away behind the house to steps leading down to a lower terrace with a large pool surrounded by comfortable lounge chairs. Overlooking the pool is a protected terrace and a cheerful blue-and-white tiled outdoor kitchen where guests may prepare a light meal. Well-tended gardens abound— the display of flowers everywhere is magnificent. In the background the property extends to a backdrop of pine and olive trees. Neither Charlotte nor Marceau speaks English, but their hospitality is so genuine that language barriers are quickly overcome. *Directions:* From the A50 (about 11 km west of Toulon), take the Bandol exit and follow signs to Le Beausset on the D359. Go through the village and take the second right at the roundabout. In about a block you see a Casino supermarket on your left and on your right a *boulangerie.* Take the tiny road beside the bakery (Chemin de Cinq-Sous) for 1.1 km. Turn left at a small lane signposted Zerbib, Marceau-Architect and continue a short distance to Les Cancades.

LES CANCADES (Gîtes de France)
Hosts: Charlotte & Marceau Zerbib
83330 Le Beausset, France
Tel: 04.94.98.76.93, Fax: 04.94.90.24.63
www.karenbrown.com/france/lescancades.html
4 rooms with private bathrooms
Double: 350F–500F
No table d'hôte
Open all year, No English spoken
Region: Côte d'Azur; Michelin Map 245

Les Tournillayres is an especially delightful bed and breakfast. Every detail—from the beautifully tended gardens to the impeccably maintained guestrooms—displays the hand of a meticulous, caring owner. There is a refreshing mood of naturalness about the property which is dotted with olive trees and green oaks, and bounded by vineyards—nothing seems stiff or formal. Your lovely hostess, Marie Claire, lives with her family on the grounds in a picture-perfect farmhouse with pink stucco exterior, pretty blue shutters, and rustic red-tiled roof. Tucked in the gardens and scented by lavender are four sweet individual cottages which, like the main house, are a pretty soft pink accented by blue shutters and doors. Each spacious cottage has been charmingly decorated in a cozy French-country style. The furnishings are similar throughout—only the fabrics and color schemes vary. All the rooms have twin beds, beamed ceiling, hand-crafted fireplace, antique tiles, a small kitchen, and a private terrace where guests enjoy the breakfast Marie Claire delivers each morning, packaged in a pretty picnic basket. *Directions:* From Carpentras take D974 northeast for 15 km to Bédoin. Go through town and continue on D974 marked to Mont Ventoux. Just as the road leaves Bédoin, watch for a tiny "Les Tournillayres" sign on your right and a service garage on your left. Turn left and continue to follow signs for "Les Tournillayres"—about 2 km from Bédoin.

LES TOURNILLAYRES (*Gîtes de France*)
Hostess: Marie Claire Renaudon
84410 Bédoin, France
Tel: 04.90.12.80.94, Fax: none
www.karenbrown.com/france/lestournillayres.html
4 cottages with private bathrooms
Double: from 450F Suite: 600F (4 persons)
Open Mar to mid-Nov, Very little English spoken
Table d'hôte: 130F per person, includes wine
Children up to 4 accepted
Region: Provence; Michelin Map 245

High in the French Alps, life in the small, remote villages remains very much unchanged from generation to generation. A stay with the Pasquier family offers a chance to experience a real slice of mountain farm-life—no frills, but plenty of old-fashioned hospitality and simple comforts. Their traditional farmhouse is found nestled in a narrow valley flanked by green meadows and jagged peaks. The region is a paradise for hikers and skiers, all of whom the Pasquiers enjoy welcoming to their home and table. Madame's table d'hôte dinners feature substantial home-cooked fare typically including soup, a main course of meat and potatoes, a selection of cheeses, green salad, and fresh fruit for dessert. Bedrooms are small but adequate with basic, yet pleasant decor each with the convenience of its own tiny bathroom. *Directions:* Bellevaux is located approximately 50 km northeast of Geneva. Take D907 from Geneva for about 35 km to the town of Saint Jeoire. Exit the national route and go into town, looking for a turnoff about halfway through town for Megevette. Continue through Megevette and look for a turnoff to the right just before the town of Bellevaux marked Chevrerie and Lac de Vallon. Pass the several chalets that make up the hamlet of Clusaz and look for a Chambres d'Hôtes sign marking a driveway on the right to the Pasquiers' farm.

CHEZ PASQUIER (Gîtes de France)
Hosts: Geneviève & Francis Pasquier
La Clusaz
74470 Bellevaux, France
Tel: 04.50.73.71.92, Fax: none
5 rooms with private bathrooms
Double: 220F
Table d'hôte: 75F per person
Open all year, No English spoken
Region: French Alps; Michelin Maps 243, 244

Le Château, although not old, is built in traditional Norman style on the site of a fortified small castle. In fact, the original tower gates are still standing and remnants of the encircling wall can still be seen. Best of all, the entrance is over a small bridge because the original moat still wraps completely around the castle. There is even a tower, although it looks quite new with modern stone work. Inside, many materials used in the construction are old, such as ceiling beams and floor tile, thus enhancing the old-world ambiance. Your gracious hostess, Maryvonne Legras, lives here with her three small poodles and several cats. She has created a homey atmosphere with plump sofas, comfortable chairs, Oriental carpets, country antique furniture, oil paintings, personal knickknacks on the tables, and abundant arrangements of colorful flowers. Stairs wind up the tower leading to three small bedrooms, each decorated with different wallpapers and color-coordinated fabrics. A sloping roof line and casement windows create a cozy ambiance. Each of the rooms has a private shower and washbasin, but all share one WC down the hallway. The price seems a little high for rooms without any private bathrooms, but plans are under way for one to be installed in one of the bedrooms. *Directions:* From Breteuil, take road D141 west. After the road leaves the forest, turn left at the first lane—this leads to the château.

LE VIEUX CHÂTEAU (Gîtes de France)
Hostess: Maryvonne Legras
27160 Bémécourt, Breteuil, France
Tel: 02.32.29.90.47, Fax: none
4 rooms with shower & washbasin, share WC
Double: 350F
Table d'hôte—sometimes on special request
Closed Jan and Feb, Very good English spoken
Region: Normandy; Michelin Map 231

Betschdorf is a picturesque, half-timbered town that has always been known for its distinctive blue-toned stoneware. Traditional pottery methods are handed down from generation to generation, and host Christian Krumeich represents the ninth generation of potters in his family. He and his artistic wife, Joelle, have installed charming guest quarters above their large pottery workshop, offering the traveler independent, stylish accommodations. Rooms are small yet very attractive, furnished in highly tasteful combinations of contemporary and antique furniture. Artful decor includes pastel upholstery, Monet prints, dried-flower arrangements, and colorful durrie rugs. The guest salon, decorated with Oriental rugs, antique furniture, well-chosen objets d'art, and bookshelves stocked with interesting reading, offers a refined, comfortable ambiance for relaxation and meals. *Directions:* Betschdorf is located approximately 44 km northeast of Strasbourg. Take N63 past Hagenau, continuing on D263 towards Hunspach and Wissembourg. After about 10 km, turn right onto D243 to Betschdorf. Soon after entering town, on the main street, look for the Krumeichs' driveway on the right, marked by a sign for Poterie and Chambres d'Hôtes.

CHEZ KRUMEICH (Gîtes de France)
Hosts: Joelle & Christian Krumeich
23, Rue des Potiers
67660 Betschdorf, France
Tel: 03.88.54.40.56, Fax: 03.88.54.47.67
www.karenbrown.com/france/chezkrumeich.html
3 rooms with private bathrooms
Double: 200F–290F
No table d'hôte
Open all year, Some English spoken by Joelle
Credit cards: VS, MC
Region: Alsace; Michelin Map 242

La Grande Métairie, a characterful 16th-century stone farmhouse, belonged to Christine Moy's grandfather. Happily, very little has been altered over the years except for the necessary modernization of plumbing and electricity. The beamed-ceilinged dining room is a gem. Its enormous fireplace, copper pots, fresh flowers, antique fruitwood sideboard, and stone floors gleaming with the patina of age are enhanced by meter-thick walls. Here Christine sets the table with a checkered cloth and serves on beautiful Limoges china. She prepares simple, yet superb meals from food grown on their organic farm—even the butter, meat, cheeses, and vegetables come from their property—and will serve vegetarian meals on request. There are two tastefully decorated bedrooms plus a two-bedroom apartment. La Grande Métairie is a simple working farm. The accommodations, ambiance, and genuine warmth of welcome far outshine the modest price (there is even a swimming pool on a back terrace and bikes for guests to use). *Directions:* Ruffec is located 147 km northeast of Bordeaux via the N10. Go to Ruffec and take D740 east towards Confolens. After the road crosses the river, take D 197 towards Bioussac, then in 1.3 km turn left towards Oyer. Soon you will see La Grande Métairie on your left. Note: Trains run from Paris to Ruffec each day (6 km from the farm).

LA GRANDE MÉTAIRIE (Gîtes de France)
Hosts: Christine & Jean Louis Moy
Oyer
16700 Bioussac, France
Tel: 05.45.31.15.67, Fax: 05.45.29.07.28
www.karenbrown.com/france/lagrandemetairie.html
2 rooms, 1 apt, with private bathrooms
Double: 225F Apt: 355F
Table d'hôte: 75F per person, includes wine
Open Apr to Nov, Very good English spoken
Region: Limousin; Michelin Map 233

Le Vieux Cognet has a prime position, directly on the edge of the River Loire. In fact, if you walk down to the river's edge and look to your left, you can see the towers of the beautiful Blois cathedral. The approach to this small bed and breakfast does not display its full potential: all you see is a house sitting directly on the road. But once you pull into the driveway, the superb setting is revealed—the cottage-like dove-gray home with gray roof is right on the banks of the Loire. In early summer, a mass of roses laces the exterior. Each of the bedrooms has a fabulous, unobstructed view. All of the individually decorated rooms have fresh, new furnishings and color-coordinated drapes and spreads. There are three guestrooms on the lower level, each with a bathroom en suite, with three more bedrooms upstairs. If you want a real bargain, ask for the tiny bedroom (just big enough to squeeze in a double bed) tucked under the eaves with a bathroom across the hall. Each morning breakfast is served either outside when the weather is warm, or else in a cozy, beamed-ceiling dining room just off the terrace. Françoise is a good cook and serves freshly baked bread, homemade jams, and just-out-of-the-oven cakes each morning. *Directions:* From Blois, follow N152 southwest along the banks of the Loire. Watch carefully on the side of the road for a Chambres d'Hôtes sign where you make a sharp left turn into the driveway of Le Vieux Cognet.

LE VIEUX COGNET (Gîtes de France)
Hostess: Françoise Cosson
4 Levée des Grouëts
41000 Blois, France
Tel: 02.54.56.05.34, Fax: 02.54.74.80.82
www.karenbrown.com/france/levieuxcognet.html
6 rooms with private bathrooms
Double: 400F–450F
No table d'hôte
Open Apr to Oct 15, Some English spoken
Region: Loire Valley; Michelin Map 238

A mountain road winds through rustic Alpine hamlets and grassy fields of wildflowers to reach the Bertrands' contemporary home. Circular in shape, the house was designed by Monsieur, an architect by trade, and built on a ridge overlooking mountain ranges on either side. Inside, all bedrooms are built around a central living area that has picture windows showing off the lovely view. Floral-print drapes bring a breath of spring into the attractive living area which contains inviting couches and a cozy fireplace. Guest bedrooms are small but comfortable and are accessible either through the Bertrands' living area or via French doors leading out to a garden and tree-covered hillside. Monsieur and Madame Bertrand and their children are friendly and solicitous hosts who also enjoy sharing home-cooked family meals with their guests. *Directions:* Bois Barbu is located about 30 km southwest of Grenoble. From Grenoble, go through Sassenage, then take D531 to Villard de Lans. Just before the village of Villard de Lans, turn right towards Cote 2000 and Corrençon. After 1 km, turn right following signs for Bois Barbu and Val Chevrière. At Bois Barbu take the left-hand fork of the road which will climb up slightly. Turn left again just before L'Auberge des Montards, then follow the winding road up to Col du Liorin and look for the Bertrands' low white house on the left.

CHEZ BERTRAND (Gîtes de France)
Hosts: Monsieur & Madame Bertrand
Bois Barbu
38250 Villard de Lans, France
Tel: 04.76.95.82.67, Fax: 04.76.95.85.75
2 rooms with private bathrooms
Double: 235F
Table d'hôte: 85F per person
Open all year, No English spoken
Region: French Alps; Michelin Map 244

The Bons' romantic Alpine cottage is found high in a meadow filled with wildflowers and bordered by dark pine trees. Dominique and Agnes are an attractive couple who have lovingly restored and decorated their 250-year-old farmhouse, adding modern comfort while accenting its rustic country charm. Agnes is a wonderfully creative cook and enjoys preparing healthy, gourmet meals for guests. We enjoyed a friendly meal with the Bons and their three children featuring a crisp green salad, a delicate pork dish made with plenty of fresh eggplant and garden tomatoes, a selection of regional cheeses, and homemade custard topped with ripe strawberries. Upstairs, bedrooms are all freshly renovated with dainty flowered wallpapers and matching coverlets, complemented by country antiques and bouquets of field flowers. Rooms are small, but guests are invited to make themselves at home in the pretty downstairs sitting room with a cozy wood stove and well-stocked bookshelves. *Directions:* Bois Barbu is located about 30 km southwest of Grenoble. From Grenoble, go through Sassenage, then take D531 to Villard de Lans. Just before the village of Villard de Lans, turn right towards Cote 2000 and Corrençon. After 1 km later turn right following signs for Bois Barbu and Val Chevrière. Continue for 3 km and turn left opposite the cross-country ski center onto the Bons' gravel driveway.

CHEZ BON (Gîtes de France)
Hosts: Dominique & Agnes Bon
Bois Barbu
38250 Villard de Lans, France
Tel: 04.76.95.92.80, Fax: 04.76.95.56.79
3 rooms with private bathrooms
Double: 280F
Table d'hôte: 90F per person
Open all year, Some English spoken
Region: French Alps; Michelin Map 244

Monsieur and Madame Letrésor, the attractive couple who own the Manoir du Champ Versant, thoroughly enjoy welcoming travelers into their 450-year-old, half-timbered manor house. It is not surprising that over the years they have built up a very faithful repeat clientele. One of their returning guests is a New York artist who visits once a year and stays for a month at a time in order to paint the surrounding countryside: his pretty watercolors are found adorning the walls of the Letrésors' home. This home is full of character inside and out. The well-kept grounds embrace wide grassy areas, a pond, miscellaneous buildings, horses, and chickens. Inside there are huge, open-hearthed stone fireplaces in both the salon and breakfast room, complemented by country antique furniture. Upstairs, the bedrooms are also very inviting with stone fireplaces, antique beds, and armoires. Our room was the smaller of the two, cozy and intimate with an ancient cupboard, convenient writing table, and window with pretty view of the garden. We highly recommend the Letrésors' picturesque home, particularly to those travelers who value authentic charm and a warm welcome over luxurious comfort. *Directions:* Bonnebosq is located about 32 km east of Caen. Three km north of Bonnebosq on D16 look for a Manoir du Champ Versant sign directing you to turn right onto a country road. Another sign marks the Letrésors' driveway to the left.

MANOIR DU CHAMP VERSANT (Gîtes de France)
Hosts: Monsieur & Madame Letrésor
Manoir du Champ Versant
14340 Bonnebosq, France
Tel and Fax: 02.31.65.11.07
2 rooms with private bathrooms
Double: 275F
No table d'hôte
Open Easter to Nov, Very little English spoken
Region: Normandy; Michelin Map 231

The Jas des Eydins is absolute perfection. Shirley Kozlowski, your lovely hostess, hails from England and Jan, her gracious husband, was born in Poland, but Paris was their home for 30 years. Deciding to move to the countryside, they found in Provence an abandoned stone farmhouse with great potential. Jan, an architect, did the stunning renovation—obviously a labor of love and talent. The reception room has a large antique trestle table where breakfast is served on chilly mornings, but usually breakfast is outside on the terrace overlooking a field of lavender. Across the courtyard (in a low stone building which used to house the sheep) are four delightful bedrooms. Each has a pretty, fresh, uncluttered look accented by a few country antiques (my favorite is the one decorated in sunny yellow and white). There is the added bonus of a sheltered terrace with an open-air kitchen where guests may fix themselves a light meal. This terrace faces a superb pool, set on a lawn dotted with olive trees and bordered by beautifully tended flowerbeds. Best of all, a vineyard (with a border of cherry trees) stretches almost to the edge of the pool. There are sweeping views in every direction—truly Provence at it finest. *Directions:* Exit the A7 at Avignon Sud following signs to Apt. After Le Coustellet, continue 15 km on the N100 to the signpost for Pont Julien. Turn right, cross over the Roman bridge, and continue on D149 towards Bonnieux. After 2 km, the sign for Jas des Eydins on your right.

JAS DES EYDINS
Hosts: Shirley & Jan Kozlowski
Route du Pont Julien
84480 Bonnieux, France
Tel: 04.90.75.84.99, Fax: 04.90.75.96.71
www.karenbrown.com/france/jasdeseydins.html
4 rooms with private bathrooms
Double: 450F–600F (3-night minimum)
No table d'hôte
Open Apr to Oct, Fluent English spoken
Region: Vaucluse; Michelin Map 245

After looking unsuccessfully to buy a bed and breakfast in England (their homeland), Eunice and Tony Doubleday expanded their horizons to France where prices were lower. Eunice said, "Location was our main concern because you can always fix up a house, but you can't change where it is." Luckily, they found an abandoned cottage with attached barns, fabulously located on the banks of the River Dronne, just a few-minutes' walk from the stunning medieval village of Brantôme. Seeing the potential, the Doubledays snatched it up. Tony did all the major work himself—plumbing, electrical, carpentry. Eunice helped tremendously with the labor and also made the curtains and stenciled designs on the walls. The cottage is now a charming two-bedroom apartment (available for long-term winter rentals at reduced rates). The adjacent barns form the bed and breakfast with a parlor and dining room and five pleasantly decorated guestrooms. Splurge and ask for number two, an especially romantic room tucked up under the sloping eaves with tall windows facing two sides—one looking to the front, the other overlooking the river. This spotless, sweet, English-style bed and breakfast offers excellent value and genuine warmth of welcome. An added bonus is the table d'hôte— Eunice prepares delicious, home-cooked meals. *Directions:* From Perigueux take the D939 north to the center of Brantôme. After the roundabout, take the second road to the right, go around the cemetery, and the bed and breakfast is signposted on your left.

LES HABRANS (Gîtes de France)
Hosts: M. Pierre Falcoz
24310 Brantôme, France
Tel: 05.53.05.58.84, Fax: none
5 rooms, 1 apt, with private bathrooms
Double: 275F–320F Apt: 1,600F–3,200F per week
Table d'hôte: 100F per person, includes wine
Closed Nov to Mar, Fluent English spoken
Region: Dordogne; Michelin Map 233

If you want to experience genuine French hospitality in a storybook château, the Château de Brie is perfection. Hosts Comte and Comtesse du Manoir de Juaye's welcome is so warm, so genuine, that you quickly feel right at home. The castle was used for many years only for holidays, but now it is the family's permanent home and although the four daughters live away, they too love the château and come home as often as possible. The rooms of the castle are elegant yet comfortable. The furnishings are gorgeous—all family antiques that have been in the castle forever. One of the most endearing qualities of this castle is that although the walls are 2 meters thick, light streams through the many windows, giving the rooms a light and cheerful ambiance. The Château de Brie is surrounded by pretty gardens and grassy lawns that stretch out behind the castle—in every direction there are tranquil views of trees and farmland. Beyond the manicured park (dominated by the picture-perfect castle) the family owns 1,000 acres of forest, a haven for walking. There are also a swimming pool and tennis courts and bicycles are available. *Directions:* Brie is located 45 km southwest of Limoges. From Limoges go southwest on N21 for 35 km. Exit at Chalus and follow the D 42 west towards Cussac. In about 8 km you see the Château de Brie well signposted on the right side of the road.

CHÂTEAU DE BRIE (Gîtes de France)
Hosts: Comte & Comtesse Pierre du Manoir de Juaye
Brie, 87150 Champagnac la Riviere, France
Tel: 05.55.78.17.52, Fax: 05.55.78.14.02
www.karenbrown.com/france/chateaudebrie.html
4 rooms with private bathrooms
Double: 550F–650F
Table d'hôte: 250F per person, includes wine
Open May to Nov (by reservations rest of year)
Fluent English spoken
Region: Limousin; Michelin Map 233

The Château de la Bourgonie combines all the ingredients to make a stay in France unforgettable: a fabulous old stone château dating back to the 14th century, breathtaking antiques, stunning decor, and a marvelously interesting history. As if this wasn't enough, the owners, Christine and Hubert de Commarque, open their hearts as well as their home to their guests. The château is a quadrangle built around a large central courtyard. One wing can either be used as a complete home with kitchen, dining room, living room, and four bedrooms (perfect for stays of a week or more) or the four bedrooms are also available on a bed and breakfast basis. When I asked Christine how long the château had been in her family, the answer was very simple, "forever." Just a short drive away, perched on a hillside above the River Dordogne, the de Commarque family owns the Château de la Poujade, an equally gorgeous home available to rent by the week. Either of the châteaux you choose offers peace and utter tranquillity near the prehistoric caves of Lascaux and the medieval town of Sarlat. *Directions:* Le Buisson is located 128 km east of Bordeaux. From Le Buisson take D25 towards Siorac. As you leave Le Buisson, take the first road to the right that goes over the railroad tracks and up the hill. When the road splits, go left. The road dead-ends at Château de la Bourgonie.

CHÂTEAU DE LA BOURGONIE
Hosts: Christine & Hubert de Commarque
Paleyrac, 24480 Le Buisson, France
Tel: 05.53.22.01.78, Fax: 05.53.27.97.67
www.karenbrown.com/france/chateaudelabourgonie.html
4 rooms with private bathrooms
Double: 750F 4-bedroom apt: 9,000F per week
No table d'hôte
Open May to Nov, Fluent English spoken
Region: Dordogne; Michelin Map 235

The Manoir des Tourpes (a beautiful, pastel-ochre manor accented by gray slate roof) is only 15 kilometers from Caen, yet sets a mood of being deep in the countryside. The lush lawn with a lazy weeping willow tree is bounded on two sides by a stone fence that is banked by beautifully tended flowerbeds. The third side of the property is traced by the River Dives. Beyond the river, open marshlands (dotted with cows and sheep) sweep to distant rolling hills. A comfortable parlor is set aside exclusively for the use of guests. Steps lead to the four attractively furnished bedrooms. My favorite is the red room: it isn't the largest, but it's ever-so-romantic. Tucked under the sloping roof, it has a beamed ceiling, pretty red carpet, double bed with patchwork quilt made by Michael's mother, and a charming antique writing desk set in front of casement windows that overlook the meandering river. The gracious owner, Michael Cassady, was born in the United States, but has lived in France for many years. He and his lovely French-born wife, Marie-Catherine, lived in Paris before moving to Normandy. The charm, ambiance, and comfort of their delightful home far exceed what you would expect for such a modest room price. *Directions:* From Paris, take exit 29b (Dozulé) off the A13, and follow signs to Troarn on the N175. At Troarn, turn right on the D95. Go 2 km to Bures-sur-Dives and follow signs to the Manoir (near the church). From Caen, take exit 30.

MANOIR DES TOURPES (*Gîtes de France*)
Hosts: Michael Cassady & Marie-Catherine Landon
Chemin de l'Église
14670 Bures-sur-Dives, France
Tel: 02.31.23.63.47, Fax: 02.31.23.86.10
E-mail: mcassady@caen.pacwan.net
www.karenbrown.com/france/manoirdestourpes.html
4 rooms with private bathrooms
Double: 280F–360F, No table d'hôte
Open all year, Fluent English spoken
Region: Normandy; Michelin Map 231

In 1975 Corinne and Régis Burckel de Tell bought a characterful 15th-century stone house facing directly onto the main street in the center of Calvisson, a very old village surrounded by vineyards just west of Nîmes. Corinne (an art historian) and Régis (an artist) were passionately committed to preserving the architecture and culture of the area and began the tremendous task of authentically restoring the mansion. Ceilings were stripped back to expose original beams, floors covered with stone slabs or terra-cotta tiles, and fireplaces brought back to working order. When finished with the construction, they furnished the house with a charming rustic simplicity. Nothing is cluttered or contrived—country antiques and natural fabrics prevail throughout. In the heart of the house is a romantic courtyard garden which is a true delight, with flowers and greenery setting off the stone walls. It is here under the stars that dinner is usually served. When the weather is chilly, guests eat family-style at one large table in a wonderful room with stone walls and arched ceiling. The bedrooms, reached by a stone slab circular staircase, are individually furnished and display the same tasteful, understated beauty. Régis, whose paintings highlight the walls throughout the house, offers week-long art classes for small groups. *Directions:* From A9, take the Nîmes Ouest, following signs on the D40 to Sommières. In 15 km you arrive at Calvisson—the house is next to the Mairie.

CHEZ BURCKEL DE TELL
Hosts: Corinne & Régis Burckel de Tell
Grand Rue 48, 30420 Calvisson, France
Tel: 04.66.01.23.91, Fax: 04.66.01.42.19
www.karenbrown.com/france/chezburckeldetell.html
6 rooms with private bathrooms
Double: 280F Suite: 350F
Table d'hôte: 75F per person, includes wine
Open all year, Very good English spoken
Credit cards: VS, AX
Region: Midi; Michelin Map 240

From the moment you enter Domaine de La Picquoterie it is apparent that this enchanting, 13th-century stone farmhouse is the home of an artist. Each view captures a well-thought-out scene, so perfect, yet so natural, it is like a painting. The charming owner, Jean-Gabriel Laloy, is an artist whose skills extend beyond his canvases. He rebuilt the long-neglected farmhouse, designed the incredibly beautiful gardens, upholstered the furniture, and sewed the drapes. As if these talents were not enough, a neighbor introduced him to needlepoint. As you enter, a massive stone fireplace sets the theme for the charming, intimate parlor with Oriental carpets accenting terra-cotta floors, massive beamed ceiling, stone walls, and a cheerful blue and yellow color scheme. Upstairs, two bedrooms display a timeless, restful decor of beiges, creams, and whites. All the materials are of natural fabrics with off-white homespun drapes and chairs, and soft-beige walls. The quiet tone-on-tone color scheme of the bedrooms is dramatically accented by the view out of the windows of colorful flowerbeds and an expanse of manicured green lawn. Jean-Gabriel's paintings are lovely, but his masterpiece is certainly the lovely home and award-winning garden he has created. For a week's stay, consider the delightful two-bedroom cottage in the grounds. *Directions:* Domaine de La Picquoterie is off the RN13 between Cherbourg and Bayeux. Exit the RN13 at Saint-Pierre du Mont D204. Afterwards, follow signs "La Picquoterie."

DOMAINE DE LA PICQUOTERIE
Host: Jean-Gabriel Laloy
14230 La Cambe, France
Tel: 02.31.92.09.82, Fax: 02.31.51.80.91, Car: 06.11.15.43.71
www.karenbrown.com/france/domainedelapicquoterie.html
2 rooms, 2-bedroom cottage, with private bathrooms
Double: 600F Cottage: 1,200F (per night for 4 persons)
No table d'hôte, No smoking, No pets
Open all year with reservations, Good English spoken
Region: Normandy; Michelin Map 231

Located in a beautiful area of wooded hills about an hour's drive southwest of Carcassonne is the fabulous 16th-century Château de Camon where Dominique du Pont welcomes guests into his home. The picture-perfect château encloses one side of Camon, a jewel of a walled medieval village which has been designated as one of prettiest in France. From the moment you walk into the impeccably groomed inner courtyard, a garden brimming with flowers, you are immersed in the romance of days gone by. This is definitely not the place to take your exuberant youngsters, but rather the kind of elegant retreat for pampering yourself for a few days. Every detail of the castle has been beautifully restored with an eye for perfection. The decor is also delightful with antiques enhancing the fairy-tale mood. An added bonus is the beautiful swimming pool, luring guests to linger on a summer day. If you want more strenuous activities, there are hiking, fishing, or prehistoric caves to explore. *Directions:* Mirepoix is located 47 km southwest of Carcassonne. From Mirepoix go south on D625 for 4 km then turn east towards Chalabre on D7. In about 10 km you will come to Camon. The château dominates the small town—you cannot miss it.

CHÂTEAU DE CAMON
Host: Dominique du Pont
Camon
09500 Mirepoix, France
Tel: 05.61.68.14.05, Fax: 05.61.68.81.56
7 rooms with private bathrooms
Double: 800F–1000F
Table d'hôte: 350F per person, includes wine
Open Easter to Nov, Fluent English spoken
Credit cards: all major
Region: Midi Pyrénées; Michelin Map 235

The Château du Foulon is an absolute dream: a beautiful small château surrounded by a 100-acre park, complete with 25 handsome peacocks and one naughty swan. Inside, the rooms without exception are furnished with exquisite antiques, many dating back to the 17th century. The essence is of a fine home, elegant, yet very comfortable, with a most appealing, lived-in ambiance—photographs of beautiful children and grandchildren prove this is indeed a family dwelling. The guestrooms, each nicely decorated with pretty wallpapers and attractive fabrics, look out over the gardens from large casement windows. In addition to the five bedrooms, there are also two charming apartments, each with its own little kitchen, bedroom, and living room. The Château du Foulon, built in 1840, is the home of Vicomte and Vicomtesse de Baritault du Carpia, who although they do not speak much English, exude a great warmth of welcome. If you want to explore the Médoc wine region, or just enjoy an interlude in the French countryside, I can think of no lovelier base: this is a place you must plan to stay for a while. In addition, one of the happiest surprises is the price, one of the best values we saw in France. *Directions:* Take D1 north from Bordeaux for about 28 km. When you reach Castelnau de Médoc, at the first traffic light turn left and almost immediately you see the sign for Château du Foulon on your left.

CHÂTEAU DU FOULON
Hosts: Vicomte & Vicomtesse de Baritault du Carpia
33480 Castelnau de Médoc, France
Tel: 05.56.58.20.18, Fax: 05.56.58.23.43
www.karenbrown.com/france/chateaudufoulon.html
5 rooms, 2 apts, with private bathrooms
Double: 450F–600F Apt: 500F–600F
No table d'hôte
Open all year, Very little English spoken
Region: Médoc; Michelin Map 233

When Lois and Terry Link decided to retire, France was a natural choice. Not only had their hearts been drawn to France for many years, but their son had married a French woman. Lois (a gourmet chef who owned a cheese shop in San Francisco) and Terry (a journalist for 20 years at the *Oakland Tribune*) bought the bakery in a picturesque village near Carcassonne. The bread-selling area is now a little cozy sitting room, very comfortable and inviting with Provençal print fabrics combined with cheerful yellow plaids. Upstairs are the guestrooms and an enclosed patio enhanced by a profusion of potted plants where breakfast is served on warm mornings. One of my favorite bedrooms has two tall windows with pretty drapes overlaying lacy curtains, a handsome antique bed, a little sitting area with two darling antique chairs with pretty print cushions, and a private bathroom. The charming ambiance throughout is one of homey, lived-in comfort—nothing fancy or overdone to contrived decorator perfection. Lois and Terry are marvelous hosts and you soon feel like friends of the family. *Directions:* Exit the A61 at Carcassonne Ouest towards Mazamet. At the fifth roundabout, take the D620 towards Caunes. Follow signs to the *Mairie* (town hall) where parking is usually available. L'Ancienne Boulangerie is about 20 meters down Rue Saint Genes.

L'ANCIENNE BOULANGERIE
Hosts: Lois & Terry Link
Rue Saint Genes
11160 Caunes-Minervois, France
Tel: 04.68.78.01.32, Fax: none
E-mail: AncienneBoulangerie@compuserve.com
www.karenbrown.com/france/lancienneboulangerie.html
5 rooms, 2 with private bathrooms
Double: 200F–300F, 2-night minimum in Aug
No table d'hôte
Open Feb to Dec, Fluent English spoken
Region: Languedoc-Roussillon; Michelin Map 235

Set in the midst of rolling, vineyard-covered hills, the Girards' gracious home offers a wonderful bed and breakfast experience. Formerly a hunting lodge built in 1700, the house is surrounded by grounds and majestic old pine and cedar trees. The ambiance of the Girards' home is one of homelike comfort enhanced by a certain refined elegance. Charming hosts Monsieur and Madame Girard are an attractive couple who delight in making visitors feel welcome. Inviting bedrooms attest to Michelle's flair for decoration, showcasing family antique furniture and harmonious wallpapers, curtains, and bedspreads. Details such as bathroom soaps, good bedside lighting, and sweet-smelling floral-print sheets add touches of personalized luxury. Bountiful breakfasts are served at a long table in the pretty dining room and include a large bowl of fresh fruits and four varieties of homemade preserves. Facing the park there is a terrace where breakfast is served out of doors in good weather. *Directions:* Chamboeuf is located 18 km southwest of Dijon. Take N74, following signs for Gevrey Chambertin. Turn right in the village of Gevrey onto D31 in the direction of Quemigny Poisot and Chamboeuf. In the village of Chamboeuf, drive to the church and turn left to arrive at the Girards' private car park.

LE RELAIS DE CHASSE (Gîtes de France)
Hosts: Monsieur & Madame Girard
21220 Chamboeuf, France
Tel: 03.80.51.81.60, Fax: 03.80.34.15.96
www.karenbrown.com/france/lerelaisdechasse.html
4 rooms with private bathrooms
Double: 400F–500F
No table d'hôte, No smoking
Open all year, Good English spoken
Region: Burgundy; Michelin Map 243

Laurence and Manu Dos Santos met in Boulder, Colorado, but their diverse backgrounds and love of travel have taken them all over the world. Laurence is from France, while her husband, Manu, has a Brazilian background. Having decided to open a bed and breakfast, given their mutual love of the mountains and the French Alps in particular, they chose to settle in Chamonix, at the foot of Mont Blanc, an incomparable setting of prestigious summits and glaciers. They bought and renovated a picture-perfect small chalet-style home with a marvelous location, just a two-minute walk from the center of Chamonix—so close that guests can easily walk into town for shopping or to eat at one of the many excellent restaurants. The decor is a combination of a few antique pieces plus modern lamps and furniture. All but two of the bedrooms have their own bathrooms (with open-style showers) and private balconies. Several of the bedrooms have extra beds that are ideal for families. The living room has a cozy nook where tables are set for breakfast and a pretty lounge area, framed by windows, where guests can relax. There is definitely a home-like ambiance throughout—you feel like a guest visiting friends. *Directions:* Upon arrival in Chamonix, follow signs to Centre Ville. Chalet Beauregard is located a few blocks above the tourist information office on the right side of the road going up the hill towards Le Brevent Lift.

CHALET BEAUREGARD (*Gîtes de France*)
Hosts: Laurence & Manu Dos Santos
182 Montée la Mollard
74400 Chamonix Mont Blanc, France
Tel & fax: 04.50.55.86.30
www.karenbrown.com/france/chaletbeauregard.html
7 rooms, 5 with private bathrooms
Double: 329F–459F
Table d'hôte (winter only): 99F per person
Open May 20 to Oct 20 & Dec 20 to May 5, Fluent English spoken
Region: Haute-Savoie; Michelin Map 244

The de Valbrays are a charming, enthusiastic, and artistic young couple who truly make their visitors feel like invited guests. Their grand home dates from 1773 and has been in François' family since 1820 when his great-great-great-grandfather, the Comte de Valbray, resided here. Old family photos and portraits abound in the gracious salons and we were impressed by François' casual friendliness. It is hard to pick a favorite bedroom, as all are furnished in keeping with the style and mood of the château; however, a bedchamber, the Rose Room, is very special: feminine in decor, it was once inhabited by François' grandmother. Also very special in their furnishings and outlook are the Lake Room and the Charles X Room. Downstairs, the parquet floors, grand chandeliers, and marble fireplaces in the public rooms attest to a very rich and elegant heritage. The elegance of a bygone era continues as guests dine at small candlelit tables which are dressed with family silver and china. There are billiards in the library and a swimming pool in the park available to guests. A stay of at least two days is recommended to fully appreciate the de Valbrays' hospitality and the ambiance of this aristocratic setting. *Directions*: From Angers (25 km) take the N162 north towards Laval. At Montreuil Juign (7½ km) take the D768 in the direction of Feneu to Champigné. Château des Briottières is signposted from Champigné, located on the D190.

CHÂTEAU DES BRIOTTIÈRES
Hosts: Hedwige & François de Valbray
Les Briottières Champigné, 49330 Champigné
Tel: 02.41.42.00.02, Fax: 02.41.42.01.55
www.karenbrown.com/france/chateaudesbriottieres.html
8 rooms with private bathrooms
Double: 840F–990F
Table d'hôte: 300F per person, includes wine
Open all year, Very good English spoken
Credit cards: all major
Region: Loire Valley; Michelin Map 232

Ferme de Launay is an enchanting 18th-century stone farmhouse draped in ivy and edged by colorful flowers. Inside, the appealing country-cottage ambiance continues. The living room is painted a deep red, setting off to perfection large floral prints and comfortable sofas and chairs grouped around a large open fireplace. Making a stay here especially outstanding is a genuine warmth of welcome enhanced by a professionalism rarely found in such a small property. This is not surprising—the owners, Bron and Jean-Pierre Schweizer are far from amateurs. Jean-Pierre, who is Swiss, grew up in the hotel business and has been involved with management of fine hotels since he was a boy. Also, he is a superb cook, creating such memorable meals that guests quickly put away any idea of going out to dine. Bron completes the capable team. Before moving to the Loire Valley, she was a very successful interior designer in Canada and her talent is self-evident—every detail of the decor is perfect. There are three cozy, individually decorated guestrooms, each with pretty wallpaper, beautiful fabrics, top-quality bedding, and excellent bathrooms. The Schweizers are extremely warm, gracious hosts who welcome guests as friends of the family. *Directions:* Follow N152 east for 9 km from Tours, then turn left in Vouvray onto the D46 towards Vernou. Before Chançay, Ferme de Launay is on your left.

FERME DE LAUNAY (Gîtes de France)
Hosts: Bron & Jean-Pierre Schweizer
37210 Chançay, France
Tel & fax: 02.47.52.28.21
www.karenbrown.com/france/fermedelaunay.html
3 rooms with private bathrooms
Double: 400F–500F, discount for 3 or more nights
Table d'hôte: 115F per person
Open all year, Fluent English spoken
No smoking house, Children accepted over 15
Region: Loire Valley; Michelin Map 238

The Marquis and Marquise de Longueil offer their château, in their family since 1742, to overnight guests understandably with great pride and out of necessity to maintain this magnificent property. Built in 1650, the Château de Boussac is surrounded by a moat and pasture land. You gain access to the château by crossing a bridge and entering under the arched doorway into a central courtyard guarded by four regal turrets. Family treasures and photographs are very much in evidence and make you realize that the decor is not staged but real. If prior arrangements have been made, you can dine with the de Longueils in their family dining room, enjoying a delicious meal served on family china. Currently there are two suites and two single rooms for overnight guests. The two suites are attractive and although not luxurious are commodious. Views from the rooms look out over the moat to surrounding gardens or pastures with grazing cattle. One cow actually peered in at us through the bathroom window as she munched on grass. *Directions*: From Montluçon travel 31 km east on N145 to Montmarault, continue northeast on the N145 a short distance in the direction of Moulins, and then head east on the D46 for 3½ km. Just past the town of Saint Marcel-en-Murat turn south on the D42. After the D42 crosses the A71, the Château de Boussac is signposted and located just a short distance off the D42 to the southwest.

CHÂTEAU DE BOUSSAC
Hosts: Marquis & Marquise de Longueil
à Target, 03140 Chantelle, France
Tel: 04.70.40.63.20, Fax: 04.70.40.60.03
E-mail: longueil@club-internet.fr
3 rooms, 2 suites, with private bathrooms
Double: 750F–1,400F
Table d'hôte: 220F–320F per person, includes wine
Open Apr to Nov 15, Good English spoken Credit cards: all major
Region: Auvergne; Michelin Map 239

The Manoir de Ponsay is a superb country farm estate surrounded by rolling pastures, fields of wheat, and pockets of woodlands. As you drive up the winding lane and arrive in front of the stately stone manor, you will be warmly greeted by your charming hosts, Madame and Monsieur de Ponsay. Upon entering their spacious home, you notice an abundance of handsome antiques, old prints, and family portraits. Nothing looks contrived nor chosen by a fancy decorator to fit the space—everything looks as if it has been there forever. It has. This lovely home has been passed down through 12 generations, from father to son, since 1644. Madame de Ponsay said with a smile, "I have one child, luckily he's a boy!" A stone staircase spirals up to the bedrooms. Four are extremely large and beautifully decorated in antiques (my favorite, Chambre Fleur, has pale-pink wallpaper setting off pretty pink-and-green floral fabric used on the bedcovers and repeated on the draperies). There are three additional less-expensive bedrooms which are very pleasant—just not as regal in size or decor. If it is an evening when table d'hôte is offered, by all means accept: the meals are outstanding. *Directions:* From the A83 (Nantes-Niort) take exit 6 and go northeast 11 km to Chantonnay. From Chantonnay take the D949b east in the direction of Poitiers. Just a few kilometers beyond Chantonnay, turn left in Saint Mars-des-Prés on a small road towards Puybelliard and follow signs to the Manoir de Ponsay.

MANOIR DE PONSAY
Hosts: Liliane & Marc de Ponsay
Saint Mars-des-Près
85110 Chantonnay, France
Tel: 02.51.46.96.71, Fax: 02.51.46.80.07
7 rooms with private bathrooms
Double: 440F–680F
Table d'hôte: 175F per person, includes wine
Open all year, Good English spoken, Credit cards: AX
Region: Pays de la Loire; Michelin Map 233

Monsieur and Madame Petit live in an atmospheric 200-year-old cottage covered by thick ivy, tucked away in a tiny country hamlet. Simone is a warm-hearted hostess who offers personal and caring hospitality. She loves plants and nature, and her home is entered through a greenhouse-like hallway festooned with vines and hanging plants. It is easy to feel comfortable and at home in the main sitting room where a cozy fireplace is surrounded by inviting couches and chairs. A bouquet of garden flowers dresses the dining-room table where guests gather for breakfast and evening meals. Madame Petit is a creative cook whose breakfasts include several varieties of homemade breads, coffee cake, and fruit in addition to the usual Continental fare. Table d'hôte dinners are relaxed, convivial meals featuring traditional yet healthful country cuisine. Small, charmingly decorated bedrooms offer a high level of comfort with good lighting, bathroom heaters, and ample storage space. *Directions:* La Chapelaude is located approximately 10 km northwest of Montluçon. Leave Montluçon on D943 towards Culan then 8 km later, before reaching the town of La Chapelaude, turn right at a service station and follow a country lane to the hamlet of Montroir. The Petits' ivy-covered cottage is one of the first houses on the left.

PETIT SIMONE (Gîtes de France)
Hostess: Simone Petit
Montroir
03380 La Chapelaude, France
Tel: 04.70.06.40.40, Fax: none
3 rooms with private bathrooms
Double: 190F
Table d'hôte: 60F per person, includes wine
Open all year, Very little English spoken
Region: Berry; Michelin Map 238

The Château de Prunoy, located relatively close to Paris yet removed from the more touristy Loire area, is a favorite retreat for Parisian artists, writers, and seekers of the good life in the country. The elegant yet comfortable château is frequented by a loyal clientele, no doubt drawn by the magnetic and charming presence of hostess Madame Josée Roumilhac. Madame seems to weave a magic spell which slows the pace and imbues all with a sense of peace and tranquillity, making sure that her guests feel at home, free to wander the lovely, antique-filled rooms and extensive grounds. A tree-shaded walk down an overgrown lane leads to two enchanted ponds preserved in their natural state, appearing as they were in the 16th century when the original castle was built. Each bedroom is unique and all are highly romantic, decorated and furnished with pleasing color schemes, lovely antiques, and Madame's real flair for design, style, and comfort. The Château de Prunoy's restaurant serves imaginative gourmet meals accompanied by attentive service. Plan to stay more than one night here to truly unwind and experience the special ambiance that is the Château de Prunoy. Besides the swimming pool on the estate, there are golf and horseback riding in the area. *Directions:* From Paris travel south on the A6 for 135 km, exiting at Joigny. Go right towards Montargis for 4 km, then turn left at a round crossing point for Prunoy-Charny (5 km).

CHÂTEAU DE PRUNOY
Hostess: Marie-Josée Roumilhac
Prunoy, 89120 Charny, France
Tel: 03.86.63.66.91, Fax: 03.86.63.77.79
11 rooms, 8 suites, with private bathrooms
Double: 700F Suite: 850F–900F
No table d'hôte; restaurant
Closed Nov to Mar, Good English spoken
Credit cards: all major
Region: Western Loire Valley; Michelin Map 238

The Château de la Poitevinière and its neighboring lavish châteaux remain as evidence of the decadent lifestyle and grandeur of the French court. Dating back over 200 years, the Château de la Poitevinière is situated 6 kilometers to the north of the medieval village of Chinon. This was a private home until 1985 when it was purchased by American friends who have impressively restored the house and incorporated every imaginable modern-day convenience. The château is furnished with antiques and art that maintain the integrity and ambiance of an 18th-century French château. There are five spacious bedrooms (each with luxurious bathroom) which open onto glorious views over the lovely twelve walled acres of park and gardens. Breakfast (a delicious presentation of croissants, homemade muffins, yogurt, and fresh fruit) is served in the sunny dining room. La Poitevinière's *chatelains*, Dianne, Karen, Nancy, and Charles, are present to provide a warm welcome, a glass of wine, and knowledgeable guidance as to what to see and where to eat in the area. This is a country house where you can experience France, but with American hosts. *Directions:* From Chinon or Tours take the D751 to the D16 (in the direction of Huismes), then north 6 km to the D118 left turn—La Poitevinière is noted by a small sign that directs you down a tree-lined drive on the right.

CHÂTEAU DE LA POITEVINIÈRE
Hosts: Dianne Barnes, Karen Normandy
Nancy & Charles Loewenberg
Huismes, 37420 Chinon, France
Tel: 02.47.95.58.40, Fax: 02.47.95.43.43
US Tel: (415)922-4795 US Fax: (415)928-2863
E-mail: mychateau@aol.com
www.karenbrown.com/france/chateaudelapoiteviniere.html
5 rooms with private bathrooms
Double: 980F No table d'hôte, No smoking
Open Apr to Dec, Fluent English spoken
Region: Loire Valley; Michelin Map 232

Surrounded by splendid vineyards, the Château de Chorey Les Beaune is an intimate beige stone castle with a festive jumble of steeply pitched tile roofs, towers, turrets and gables. A stone wall surrounds the property creating a secluded park that includes three 13th-century round towers. Inside, the ambiance is one of a comfortable, lived in home—no contrived, decorator-inspired decor. On the ground floor is a small breakfast room opening to a terrace where breakfast is served on warm days. To the right is the original kitchen where hunting trophies adorn the wall above the fireplace and jam is often simmering on the stove. The guestrooms, which are located upstairs, are individually decorated as in a private home. My favorite, number 4, captures incredible views of the vineyyards. François Germain's great-grandfather purchased this fabulous estate over 100 years ago (his initials are entwined in an intricate design in the tower suite). Guests are a sideline to the hospitable Germain family—their primary business is the production of wine from the château's vast estate (75,000 bottles of fine quality wines are aged in the cellars below the castle). *Directions:* From Beaune, take N74 north towards Dijon. After 2 km turn right at the sign for Chorey. Just before entering the village, you will see the château signposed on your left.

CHÂTEAU DE CHOREY LES BEAUNE (Gîtes de France)
Hosts: Family Germain
Rue Jacques-Germain
21200 Chorey Les Beaune, France
Tel: 03.22.06.05, Fax: 03.80.24.03.93
www.karenbrown.com/france/chateaudechoreylesbeaune.html
6 rooms with private bathrooms
Double: 730–850F Suite for 4: 1150F
No table d'hôte
Open Apr to Dec, Fluent English spoken
Credit cards: MC, VS
Region: Burgundy: MichelinMap 243

Chorey les Beaune is close to Beaune, a picturesque medieval town in the heart of the Côte d'Or (one of France's finest wine-producing regions). Well-known for its gourmet cuisine and fine wines, the region is a popular destination for foreign and French tourists alike, so it is a pleasure to find a good lodging value. Chez Deschamps offers modern comfort, a high level of cleanliness, and the independence of hotel accommodation combined with the warm, personalized atmosphere of a bed and breakfast. Bedrooms are all fresh and new, with thick carpeting, ample closet space, good lighting, and spotless private bathrooms. Hostess Marie-Claire Deschamps is a friendly, energetic hostess who thoughtfully provides guests with soap, tissues, and even cotton balls, and is happy to help guests plan sightseeing expeditions in the region. Guest accommodation is found in a house completely separate from the Deschamps' home. Guests have their own home-like breakfast nook and sitting room with full bookshelves and a television. *Directions:* Chorey les Beaune is located about 5 km northeast of Beaune. Take N74 towards Dijon, turning right towards Chorey les Beaune after about 1 km. Just as you enter the village, take the first left and look for a Chambres d'Hôtes sign on the gatepost of the fourth house on the left. The contemporary stucco house in front is the guest house.

CHEZ DESCHAMPS (Gîtes de France)
Hosts: Monsieur & Madame Deschamps
15, Rue d'Aloxe-Corton
Chorey Les Beaune, 21200 Beaune, France
Tel: 03.80.24.08.13, Fax: 03.80.24.08.01
www.karenbrown.com/france/chezdeschamps.html
6 rooms with private bathrooms
Double: 240F
No table d'hôte
Open Mar to Dec, No English spoken
Region: Burgundy; Michelin Map 243

Le Coin Savoyard is located in the heart of Combloux, just across the street from the church. Even without seeing the date of 1819 engraved in the stone above the front door, it is obvious this charming little hotel is quite old. It looks as if it was once a farmhouse, and indeed it was. The home belonged to Colette Astay's grandfather who not only had a farm, but ran an informal little bar where the locals could have a drink after a day of work. Colette's parents expanded the bar into a restaurant with a few rooms, and now Colette and her husband Philippe have greatly upgraded the property. Although it is still a simple hotel, the bedrooms now are very pretty. All are wood paneled and have matching bedspreads and drapes in pretty Provençal fabrics with a color scheme that varies from room to room. The dining room continues the same country look. It makes no pretense to be decorator ect, but rather exudes a refreshing quality of "realness" so often missed when interior designers try to make things too cute. There is a set dinner menu which varies each day, featuring regional specialties and local wines in a very reasonably priced four-course meal. Another bonus is that behind the hotel is a large swimming pool. *Directions:* From Chamonix take A40 west to the Sallanches exit. From Sallanches take N212 south towards Megève. In about 7 km you come to a sign for Combloux.

LE COIN SAVOYARD
Hosts: Colette & Philippe Astay
74920 Combloux, France
Tel: 04.50.58.60.27, Fax: 04.50.58.64.44
10 rooms with private bathrooms
Double: from 464F
No table d'hôte; restaurant
Open Jun to Oct & Nov to Apr, Some English spoken
Credit cards: VS
Region: Haute Savoie; Michelin Map 244

A half-timbered exterior, overflowing windowboxes, and a wheelbarrow full of flowers in the front yard of this 250-year-old farmhouse only hint at the country charm found inside. Madame Anfrey is an energetic farmwife who, when not bustling about making sure her guests feel at home, helps her husband tend their cows and poultry. Madame's artistic nature is evident in the very cozy and pleasantly cluttered feeling she has achieved throughout her farm cottage. The guest bedrooms are all charmingly decorated with a variety of antiques, dried-flower arrangements, and old paintings. Breakfast is served at a round table in the main room supervised by an old grandfather clock in the corner. The low, beamed ceilings, hanging copper pots, country antiques, and cozy fire on rainy days make this a tempting spot to linger over café au lait, tea, or hot chocolate served in country pottery. We were sad indeed to leave this quaint, friendly bed and breakfast. *Directions:* Conteville is located approximately 60 km west of Rouen via A13 to the Beuzeville exit, then N175 to N178 to Foulbec, then D312 to Conteville. There are several Chambres d'Hôtes advertised by roadside signs in the vicinity of Conteville, so be sure to follow those in the direction of Le Clos Potier. The route involves several turns, but is very well signposted, and you will find the farmhouse tucked away on a country road behind a white fence.

LA FERME DU PRESSOIR (Gîtes de France)
Hosts: Odile & Pierre Anfrey
Conteville, 27210 Beuzeville, France
Tel & Fax: 02.32.57.60.79
www.karenbrown.com/france/lafermedupressoir.html
5 rooms with private bathrooms
Double: 260F
Table d'hôte: 120F per person
Open all year, Very little English spoken
Region: Normandy; Michelin Map 231

La Butte de L'Épine is a jewel. Although the long, low stone and stucco building reflects the local style of architecture from the 17th century, the building is not old. It was designed and built by Michel Bodet who cleverly incorporated all the best of past and present into this beautiful home. Although the building oozes charm, it is the interior that makes this home so special. Michel's wife, Claudette, combines a love of flowers with an artistic flair for decorating. The home abounds with exquisite large floral arrangements which set off to perfection the patina of many country antiques. The spacious living/dining room looks out to a manicured garden and beyond to a small wood. A private guest entrance leads to two cozy guestrooms tucked up under the eaves. Both rooms are intimately charming, but my favorite is the corner room with windows on two walls. Delicate green wallpaper with a tiny rose pattern covering the sloping walls and ceiling, pink bedspreads, and pretty pink floral material for the drapes and tablecloth create a decorator-perfect scheme. You cannot help being enchanted with the thoughtfulness of every detail including pink candy and pink flowers by the bedside: an oasis to return to after a day of châteaux excursions in the Loire Valley. *Directions:* From Bourgueil, take D749 north for 12 km to Gizeux. Turn right (east) on D15 and continue to Continvoir. At the church, turn left on D64. La Butte de l'Épine is less than 1 km along on your right.

LA BUTTE DE L'ÉPINE (*Gîtes de France*)
Hosts: Claudette & Michel Bodet
37340 Continvoir, France
Tel and fax: 02.47.96.62.25
www.karenbrown.com/france/labuttedelepine.html
2 rooms with private bathrooms
Double: 320F
No table d'hôte
Closed Christmas, No English spoken
Region: Loire Valley; Michelin Map 232

Usually the places to stay that we suggest are quite old, filled with historical ambiance. Not so with La Rabouillère—it is new. The home was designed by the owner, Jean Marie, who actually built it himself on weekends. There is a story-book quality to this brick and timbered bed and breakfast with a steeply pitched roof accentuated by perky gables. You enter into a large family room where guests gather before the open fire in the winter. Antiques abound, and with the beamed ceiling, timber and exposed brick walls, the mood is certainly old world. This family/living room is where Martine serves breakfast on chilly mornings, although when the days are balmy guests frequently prefer to eat outside. Martine lovingly decorated each bedroom with Laura-Ashley-type fabrics and antique accent pieces. The rooms are all named after flowers. My favorite, Les Jonquilles, is decorated in soft yellows. All of the bathrooms are spacious and offer special amenities such as built-in hairdryers. In addition to the five bedrooms, there is a two-bedroom apartment. The setting too is superb: a 17-acre wooded estate with a small pond in front. For those who are château sightseeing, La Rabouillère is right in the heart of the Loire Valley. *Directions:* Go south from Blois on D765 for about 9 km to Cour-Cheverny then take D102 towards Contres. About 6 km beyond Cheverny, turn left following the La Rabouillère signs.

LA RABOUILLÈRE (Gîtes de France)
Hostess: Martine Thimonnier
Chemin de Marçon
41700 Contres, France
Tel: 02.54.79.05.14, Fax: 02.54.79.59.39
www.karenbrown.com/france/larabouillere.html
5 rooms, 2-bedroom apartment, with private bathrooms
Double: 360F–550F Apt: 800F
No table d'hôte
Open all year, Some English spoken, Credit cards: all major
Region: Loire Valley; Michelin Map 238

Upon Dennis's retirement from the British Diplomatic Service, the Thornleys decided for the first time in their lives to put down roots. They bought a characterful 13th-century watchtower with an extraordinary setting on a slope just below Cordes-sur-Ciel, classified as one of France's most beautiful villages. The Thornleys meticulously restored the property which looks out to a sweeping view of the valley. Capturing the same view is a large swimming pool which guests are welcome to use. There are four sweetly decorated, meticulously tidy guestrooms, each with its own entrance and flowered balcony or patio where breakfast is served. Cordes has many restaurants but, for those who prefer to "eat in," there is a summer kitchen with a refrigerator and barbecue where guests may fix a meal. For such reasonably priced accommodations, the amenities are outstanding—including large bars of soap that far surpass those often found in deluxe hotels. However, the great merit of this small bed and breakfast is the genuine, unpretentious friendliness of the Thornleys. As Dennis said, they are doing almost what they did for many years in the diplomatic service—just on a more personal level. *Directions:* Upon arrival in lower Cordes, take the cobbled street up the hill at the "Cité" sign. After 500 meters, take the left fork down the hill, marked with two small sighs "Le Bouysset" and "Aurifat." Aurifat is signposted on your right, about 200 meters after a hairpin curve.

AURIFAT (Gîtes de France)
Hosts: Patricia & Dennis Thornley
Aurifat, 81170 Cordes-sur-Ciel, France
Tel: 05.63.56.07.03, Fax: none
www.karenbrown.com/france/aurifat.html
2 rooms with private bathrooms, 2-room suite with bathroom
Double: 260F Suite: 480F (4 persons), discount for 7 nights
No table d'hôte, No Children
Open Easter to Dec, Fluent English spoken
Region: Midi-Pyrenees; Michelin Map 235

Susanna McGrath, who is Scottish, was looking for a place with character in the Loire Valley where she could open a bed and breakfast. When she discovered the beautiful 15th-century Le Logis du Sacriste, located in the quaint village of Cormery, she bought it in three days. The house is adjacent to, and was originally part of, Cormery's historic abbey. The abbey still forms one wall of Susanna's idyllic enclosed garden where dinner is served on balmy evenings. Susanna has brought her own abundant charm and style to the home. She covered the floors in antique terra-cotta tiles, added a fireplace in the lounge, and draped the windows in ever-so-pretty English fabrics. The renovations added all the needed ingredients for guests' comfort without losing the authentic heritage of the house. A narrow wooden staircase still circles up to charming guestrooms. One of my favorites is a romantic room tucked under the eaves which is decorated with pretty green-and-white plaid fabric. The house is simple but exudes the refinement and good taste of your charming hostess, who is also an exceptional cook and for many years had a successful catering business in London. *Directions:* Take the N12 south from Tours then join the N143 and continue on to Cormery (total of about 22 km from Tours). After crossing over the bridge which marks the boundary of Cormery, the Rue Alcuin is the third road on the left after the bridge.

LE LOGIS DU SACRISTE (Gîtes de France)
Hostess: Susanna McGrath
3 Rue Alcuin, 37320 Cormery, France
Tel: 02.47.43.08.23, Fax: 02.47.43.05.48
www.karenbrown.com/france/logisdusacriste.html
5 rooms with private bathrooms
Double: 290F–330F
Table d'hôte: 140F per person, includes wine
Open Apr to Oct, Fluent English spoken
Credit cards: MC, VS
Region: Loire Valley; Michelin Map 238

Renaud Gizardin inherited the Moulin de Marsaguet, a picturesque, 200-year-old stone mill hugging the edge of a pretty little lake, from his grandparents. He lives here with his young wife, Valerie, their adorable little girl, Camille, several friendly dogs, and a cat (plus a menagerie of other "friends"—horses, ducks, chickens, and cows). There is nothing fancy about the Gizardins' well-managed bed and breakfast, but a sense of gentle goodness permeates their home. When the weather is warm, Valerie serves dinner outside family-style on a picnic table. The hearty meals are prepared totally from ingredients from their property, including the foie gras. The prune liqueur served at the end of the meal is made by Valerie's grandfather. A narrow staircase leads up to the bedrooms. My favorite, the sweetly old-fashioned corner room, has a pretty pink floral wallpaper, a wooden floor, fresh flowers on the small desk, antique headboard on the double bed, armoire, and a good-sized, sparkling clean bathroom. Casement windows on two walls open out to the farm, making this room especially bright and cheerful. This modestly priced farm is about as far from the bustle of civilization as you can get. Just stretch out under a tree, hike, or row your way to the middle of the lake and watch the wild ducks. *Directions:* From Limoges take D704 south to Saint Yrieix. Then east for 10 km to Coussac Bonneval where you look for the Chambres d'Hôtes signs directing you to the bed and breakfast, about 2 km from town.

MOULIN DE MARSAGUET (Gîtes de France)
Hosts: Valerie & Renaud Gizardin
87500 Coussac-Bonneval, France
Tel: 05.55.75.28.29, Fax: none
www.karenbrown.com/france/moulindemarsaguet.html
3 rooms with private bathrooms
Double: 240F
Table d'hôte: 90F per person, includes wine
Open all year (winter by reservation), Good English spoken
Region: Limousin; Michelin Map 239

The Chauveaus are antique dealers who have seasoned their expertise and good taste with a touch of whimsy to create wonderfully imaginative decor and furnishings in their 250-year-old home. Do not expect to see the same antique pieces on a second visit, however, as Monsieur Chauveau is fond of pointing out that all furniture is for sale and therefore subject to change. We stayed in a charming attic room with beautiful exposed support beams and an adjoining immaculate bathroom thoughtfully stocked with ample toiletries and luxurious fluffy towels. Floor-level windows overlook the prettily landscaped swimming pool. The most outstanding bedroom is a corner suite decorated in tones of lavender, green, and yellow with windows (even from the enormous bathroom) looking out over the vineyards. The Chauveaus pay great attention to detail and serve an elegant breakfast complete with gold-trimmed china, silver service, and a white linen tablecloth. Contented appetites are assured after beginning the day with an artful display of exotic fruits, warmed croissants, fresh bread, homemade preserves, rich cheese, and country butter. *Directions:* Cravant les Côteaux is located 8 km east of Chinon. Take D21 through Cravant les Côteaux in the direction of Panzoult. Two km after leaving Cravant, look for a sign advertising Pallus, Bernard Chauveau, and then take the next driveway on the right.

DOMAINE DE PALLUS (Gîtes de France)
Hosts: Barbara & Bernard Chauveau
Pallus, Cravant Les Côteaux
37500 Chinon, France
Tel: 02.47.93.08.94, Fax: 02.47.98.43.00
www.karenbrown.com/france/domainedepallus.html
2 rooms, 1 suite, with private bathrooms
Double: 450F–500F Suite: 500F–600F
No table d'hôte
Open all year, Fluent English, German spoken by Madame
Region: Loire Valley; Michelin Map 232

Crillon le Brave, a walled hilltop village, is composed of a pretty, small church and a cluster of weathered stone houses. One of these houses, the Clos Saint-Vincent, has been completely renovated and is now a delightful bed and breakfast. Guests enter through large iron gates into a spacious parking area in front of a typical tan-stone building with brown shutters and tiled roof. A large swimming pool on the terrace captures a sweeping view of the surrounding countryside. There is a very attractive lounge for guests with whitewashed walls, tiled floors, a snug nook with a few comfortable chairs for reading, and a large wooden table for dining. The five bedrooms are all very similar in decor with tiled floors, small table and chairs, and color-coordinated, Provençal-style fabrics used as dust ruffles, chair cushions, and drapes. The feeling is very fresh, uncluttered, and pretty. *Directions:* Carpentras is located 24 km northeast of Avignon. From Carpentras take D974 northeast towards Bédoin then after about 10 km, follow road signs to Crillon le Brave. As the road climbs the hill towards the old village, you see the sign for Clos Saint-Vincent. Turn right at the sign and continue on a small road for about 200 meters. Turn left and continue up the hill. The Clos Saint Vincent is the second driveway on the left.

CLOS SAINT-VINCENT (*Gîtes de France*)
Hostess: Françoise Vazquez
Les Vergers
84110 Crillon Le Brave, France
Tel: 04.90.65.93.36, Fax: 04.90.12.81.46
www.karenbrown.com/france/clossaintvincent.html
5 rooms with private bathrooms
1 cottage suite for 4 persons
Double: 430F–480F Suite: 770F–970F
Table d'hôte: 140F per person, includes wine
Open all year (groups in winter), Some English spoken
Region: Provence; Michelin Maps 245, 246

It is not often that you can actually reside in a historical monument, but you can do just that at Le Prieuré Saint Michel. When Anne and Pierre Chahine bought the property, it had been sadly neglected but, happily for the lucky traveler, the complex has been authentically restored and is truly a masterpiece. The granary is now used for various exhibitions and concerts, the giant press where the monks produced the Calvados brandy is still intact, and the lovely little chapel is now an art galley featuring the sketches of one of France's great artists, Edgar Chahine, who just happens to be the father of your congenial host. Equally outstanding are the splendid, meticulously tended gardens. There is an old-fashioned rose garden featuring an incredible variety of fragrant roses from days of yore. In contrast there is the "new" rose garden, the iris garden, the herbal gardens, and on and on. Each is laid out as they would have been in the days of old. Two ponds with ducks and swans complete the idyllic scene. In summer, the grounds are open to the public, but guests are assured of their privacy with their own intimate little garden. Each of the bedrooms is handsomely decorated. *Directions:* Take D916 west from Vimoutiers towards Argentan. Just a few kilometers after leaving Vimoutiers, turn right at the sign for Crouttes. Go through town following signs for Le Prieuré Saint Michel.

LE PRIEURÉ SAINT MICHEL (Gîtes de France)
Hosts: Anne & Pierre Chahine
61120 Crouttes, Vimoutiers, France
Tel: 02.33.39.15.15, Fax: 02.33.36.15.16
2 rooms with private bathrooms
Double: 400F–500F
No table d'hôte
Open all year, Fluent English spoken
Credit cards: VS
Region: Normandy; Michelin Map 231

Madame Poulain de Saint-Père lives in a picturesque house in the village of Dangu. She speaks fluent English and takes great pleasure in helping her guests plan sightseeing excursions in the surrounding countryside. Les Ombelles dates from around 1700, yet the two guest bedrooms (reached by a private stairway independent of the rest of the house) are comfortably spacious (not always the case in older houses). The decor is an artfully conceived mélange of antiques, old etchings, and pleasing color schemes. In one of the rooms the bed is found behind a pretty flowered curtain—an intimate, delightfully French touch. Downstairs there is a cozy salon with a fireplace where guests are invited to relax with an aperitif before enjoying a lively table d'hôte dinner with Madame Poulain de Saint-Père. Breakfast is often served under a canopy on the terrace which has a peaceful view over Madame's well- flowers. A path leads through the garden to the shady banks of the River Ept where a strategically placed bench provides a tranquil spot for an afternoon of reading or quiet contemplation. *Directions:* Dangu is 60 km northwest of Paris via A15, changing to N14 to Bordeaux Saint Clair, then D146 to Dangu. In Dangu, look for a Chambres d'Hôtes sign directing you to a cream-colored house with green shutters, located just next to the bridge over the river.

LES OMBELLES (*Gîtes de France*)
Hostess: Mme Poulain de Saint-Père
4, Rue de Gue
27720 Dangu, France
Tel: 02.32.55.04.95, Fax: 02.32.55.59.87
E-mail: vextour@aol.com
www.karenbrown.com/france/lesombelles.html
3 rooms, 2 with private bathrooms
Double: 220F–330F, discount for stays 3 days or more
Table d'hôte: 130F per person
Open Mar 15 to Dec 15, Fluent English spoken
Region: Normandy; Michelin Map 231

Windowboxes full of multi-colored flowers decorate the pretty, welcoming façade of Doris Engel-Geiger's chalet-style house. Madame Geiger is a friendly hostess who keeps her home and guestrooms in spotless condition, with pretty, feminine touches such as lace-trimmed pillowcases and sheets. Furnishings are antique reproductions and rooms are small, but very comfortable. Guests are encouraged to relax in the cozy and inviting sitting room which has a stone fireplace flanked by leather chairs and picture windows looking out over distant hills. La Maison Fleurie is found in a beautiful valley dotted with small villages and fields of cherry trees. This is a region of kirsch production and each town has its own distillery where the "water of life" is made from locally grown cherries. *Directions:* Dieffenbach au Val is located approximately 30 km northwest of Colmar. Take N83 towards Strasbourg, turning left at Selestat onto N59 towards Saint Die. After 3 km, turn right onto D424 towards Ville and at the village of Saint Maurice turn left following signs for Dieffenbach. Take the next left and then look for a Chambres d'Hôtes sign marking the Geigers' chalet-style house which is set back from the road behind a front garden.

LA MAISON FLEURIE (Gîtes de France)
Hostess: Doris Engel-Geiger
19, Rue de Neuve Eglise
67220 Dieffenbach au Val, France
Tel: 03.88.85.60.48, Fax: 03.88.85.60.48
3 rooms with private bathrooms
Double: 240F–260F
No table d'hôte
Open all year, No English spoken, Fluent German
Region: Alsace; Michelin Map 242

If you want to experience a bed and breakfast at a simple, real working farm, the characterful Le Temple is a good choice. In days gone by this was the farm of the Templers, the knights of the religious order who went to the crusades, and (if you look carefully) in one wing of the courtyard you can still see the Gothic windows of a 12th-century church. Inside, you do not find decorator-perfect rooms nor antique decor, but you do experience genuine country hospitality from Chantal and Michel Le Varlet. After entering from the courtyard, there is a simple parlor where in the evening dinner is served family-style at one large table. Here guests can also read or watch television. During the day the choice place to relax is in the enormous walled garden in the rear. There are four guestrooms reached by a hallway with plastic wallpaper. Although the decor is not outstanding, the rooms are immaculately clean and each has a nice bathroom (and the price is reasonable for those on a budget). Chantal is a very good cook and in the evenings prepares hearty, delicious traditional meals using fresh produce from the farm. *Directions:* Coming from Paris, take the Dormans exit from the A4 and turn right on the RD980 towards Dormans. Stay on this road, and in a few minutes (before you reach Passy Grigny) you see the Gîtes de France sign for Le Temple on your right.

LE TEMPLE (Gîtes de France)
Hosts: Chantal & Michel Le Varlet
Passy Grigny, 51700 Dormans, France
Tel: 03.26.52.90.01, Fax: 03.26.52.18.86
www.karenbrown.com/france/letemple.html
4 rooms with private bathrooms
Double: 300F
Table d'hôte: 120F per person
Open all year, Some English spoken
Region: Champagne; Michelin Map 237

The Château d'Ecutigny, set in a serene area of gently rolling hills, is a lovely beige-stone home with turrets and a red-tile roof. However, when Françoise and Patrick Rochet bought the property in 1990, it had been sadly neglected for 150 years. The roof had collapsed, the walls had tumbled in, and sheep were the only guests on the premises—the Rochets had to promise to build a new home for them to complete the sale. The renovation is truly astounding, particularly when you realize that Patrick did all the work himself, except for placing the roof beams. Françoise was also totally involved. In addition to helping with the renovations, she did the interior design and sewed all of the drapes and bedspreads. Today the castle, whose foundation dates to the 12th century, is returned to its former glory, even better than before. Now you have running water, central heating, electricity, and private bathrooms for each of the individually decorated guestrooms (my favorite, Parquet, an enormous corner room with stunning views, has a bathroom as large as a normal bedroom). The castle has dungeons, secret passages, and even a 12th-century kitchen where Patrick sometimes makes bread in the ancient bread oven. *Directions:* From Beaune take the D970 for 20 km through Bligny/Ouche. Just after leaving town, turn left on the D33, signposted Ecutigny. Just at the end of Ecutigny, turn right towards Bessey la Cour and the castle is on your right.

CHÂTEAU D'ECUTIGNY (Gîtes de France)
Hosts: Françoise & Patrick Rochet
Ecutigny, 21360 Bligny-sur-Ouche, France
Tel: 03.80.20.19.14, Fax: 03.80.20.19.15
www.karenbrown.com/france/chateaudecutigny.html
6 rooms with private bathrooms
Double: 500F–700F Suite: 700F–1,000F
Table d'hôte: 230F per person, includes wine
Open all year, Very good English spoken
Credit cards: all major
Region: Burgundy; Michelin Map: 243

L'Esclériade is a contemporary home that reflects the characteristics of the marvelous old farmhouses dotting the landscape of Provence—the façade is a pale-peach color, the shutters blue, and the roof of heavy red tile. From the flower gardens to the interior rooms, everything is immaculate and well kept. Pride of ownership is displayed throughout, and Marie-Jeanne and Vincent Gallo take the same special care of their guests as they do their home. Though neither speaks very much English, their hospitality is spontaneous. Each of the bedrooms is individual in decor, but similar in ambiance with simple modern furniture, and curtains and spreads with a country-Provençal motif. Four of the six bedrooms enjoy a private terrace and my favorites are those whose terraces enjoy the lovely view across the valley. Fronting the house is a patio with white tables and chairs shaded by umbrellas and large pots of red geraniums. Steps from the patio lead down to a lower terrace where a large swimming pool is surrounded by a lush lawn. *Directions:* Exit the A7 (Orange to Aix en Provence) at Avignon north and follow signs to Carpentras. From Carpentras go north on D938. Past Malaucène watch for the road to the right to Entrechaux. L'Esclériade is not in the village, but located outside on the road to Saint Marcellin les Vaison.

L'ESCLÉRIADE (Gîtes de France)
Hosts: Marie-Jeanne & Vincent Gallo
Route de Saint-Marcellin
84340 Entrechaux, France
Tel: 04.90.46.01.32, Fax: 04.90.46.03.71
www.karenbrown.com/france/lescleriade.html
6 rooms with private bathrooms
Double: 320F–360F
Table d'hôte: 110F per person
Open Mar to Nov, Very little English spoken
Credit cards: MC, VS
Region: Provence; Michelin Map 245

Les Patrus, a simple 16th-century farmhouse set in the Champenoise countryside, is conveniently close to Paris by car or train and within an easy drive of Euro Disneyland. Les Patrus' stucco-covered stone buildings form a square, completely enclosing a central grassy courtyard. One of the most popular places in the house is a magnificent dining room dominated by a large fireplace. Here you find five comfortable white sofas and a large dining table that seats up to 20 people. In this welcoming room, furnished with antiques and with large windows to welcome the sun, guests gather to eat and share their experiences of the day. Adjacent to the dining room is a bright hall with wooden stairs leading the way up to a library on the mezzanine. To the right of the library is the Berry suite made up of two bedrooms and a shared bathroom—a perfect setup if traveling with children. My favorite room, the Poitou, looks out over the tiled roofs to rolling fields and a tranquil pond. Mary Ann runs Les Patrus with warmth and efficiency—she has a gift of making her guests feel genuinely at home. An added bonus is her fluent English—not surprising as her father (a Texan) returned to France after World War II to marry his French sweetheart. *Directions:* From the A4, take the Saint Jean/Les Deux Jumeaux exit and head east on D407 and D933 towards Montmirail to the village of La Haute Épine. Turn right towards L'Épine aux Bois. Les Patrus is 500 meters on your right.

LES PATRUS (*Gîtes de France*)
Hosts: Mary Ann & Marc Royol
02450 L'Épine aux Bois, France
Tel: 03.23.69.85.85, Fax: 03.23.69.98.49
3 rooms, 3 suites, with private bathrooms
Double: 300F–490F Suite: 500F–590F
Table d'hôte: 130F–150F per person, includes wine
Open all year, Fluent English spoken
Credit cards: VS, MC
Region: Champagne; Michelin Map 237

At the heart of the Loire Valley, the Manoir du Grand Martigny is a perfect base for touring the château country. In addition to a superb location, the Manoir offers hosts who speak fluent English, comfort, charm, and a warm welcome—all at a reasonable price. The Desmarais have refurbished every nook and cranny of their spacious home so the roomy bedrooms are in tiptop condition and each is accompanied by a luxurious bathroom. Two of the bedrooms have an adjoining children's room that makes them ideal for families. Breakfast is served family-style at a huge table in front of a large rustic fireplace in a room that adjoins the beautiful country kitchen. When the house is full of guests, places are also set in the formal dining room. A courtyard at the back, overlooked by its own turret, is a tranquil place for a morning croissant. There is a game room for children who aren't yet tired after a day of châteaux-hopping. The Desmarais provide a wealth of information on the surrounding châteaux that are open to the public. For dining there are restaurants to suit all budgets within a few minutes' drive. *Directions:* From Paris, leave the A10 at the Tours North exit. Continue through town to the Loire. Do not cross the river but turn to the right on the north bank, following N152 in the direction of Langeais. The Manoir, signposted as Chambres d'Hôtes, is located on the north side directly off the N152 just 4 km from Tours.

MANOIR DU GRAND MARTIGNY
Hosts: Monique & Henri Desmarais
Vallières, 37230 Fondettes, France
Tel: 02.47.42.29.87, Fax: 02.47.42.24.44
5 rooms with private bathrooms
Double: 460F–700F Suite: 980F (2-night minimum)
No table d'hôte
Open Apr to Nov 15, Fluent English spoken
Region: Loire Valley; Michelin Map 232

Le Domaine de Mestré, a former agricultural estate belonging to the Fontevraud Abbey, dates back to the 12th century. Its origins are even older—stones in the courtyard show traces of an ancient Roman road. You enter through gates into the courtyard. Immediately to your left is a pretty tithe barn which now houses an attractive boutique featuring beautifully packaged soaps and bath oils (sold under the trade name of Martin de Candre). These are manufactured right on the property by three generations of the Dauge family. Because all their products are without any artificial coloring, fragrances, or chemicals, they are very popular—some even exported to the United States. Across the courtyard from the boutique, the 12th-century chapel has been converted into the dining room, attractively decorated with yellow walls and small tables set with yellow linens. The bedrooms are in two separate stone buildings which also face onto the courtyard. Although not deluxe, all of the bedrooms are attractive and most have antique furniture and feature Laura Ashley fabrics. The gracious Dauge family strive to make each guest feel welcome in their home. Rosine prepares lovely meals using ingredients from the estate farm. *Directions:* Take the N152 (Tours to Samur) and cross the river to Montsoreau. From Montsoreau take D947 towards Fontevraud l'Abbaye. Soon after leaving Montsoreau (before reaching the town of Fontevraud-l'Abbaye), you see the sign where you turn right for Le Domaine de Mestré.

LE DOMAINE DE MESTRÉ
Hosts: Rosine & Dominique Dauge
49590 Fontevraud l'Abbayè, France
Tel: 02.41.51.75.87, Fax: 02.41.51.71.90
12 rooms with private bathrooms
Double: 395F
Table d'hôte: 140F per person
Open Apr to Dec 20, open weekends only Feb & Mar
Very good English spoken by son-in-law
Region: Loire Valley; Michelin Map 232

Located in the sweet village of Fontvieille (just minutes from Les Baux, Saint Remy, and Arles), Mas de la Tour is truly an outstanding find. High stone walls surround the grounds so it is not until you enter the gates that the stunning beauty of the property is revealed—a romantic, picture-perfect 17th-century home with rustic tiled roof and dark-green shutters. The house is surrounded by a gorgeous, perfectly tended garden, and nestled in one corner of the lush, tree-dotted lawn is a splendid swimming pool. Inside there are five large guestrooms, each individually decorated. There is not a hint of commercialism—it truly feels as if you are a lucky guest in a private home. However, behind the scenes every tiny detail for guests' comfort has been well thought out (the bedrooms even have direct-dial telephones). Your charming hostess, Madame Burnet, is no amateur—before opening Mas de la Tour, she owned many large resort hotels. Monique is also a fabulous cook and one of our readers reported that he had the best meal in all of France at her table. *Directions:* As you come into Fontvieille on the D33 from Tarascon, do not turn into the town center, but continue straight ahead. On your right you will pass Hostellerie de la Tour. Soon after, you come to La Tour des Abbés on your right. Opposite La Tour des Abbés, turn left onto Rue de la Tour and look for number 13.

MAS DE LA TOUR
Hostess: Monique Burnet
13, Rue de la Tour
13990 Fontvieille, France
Tel: 04.90.54.76.43, Fax: 04.90.54.76.50
www.karenbrown.com/france/masdelatour.html
5 rooms with private bathrooms
Double: 400F–500F
Table d'hôte: 150F per person, includes wine
Open all year, Some English spoken
Region: Provence; Michelin Map 245

If you are looking for a château whose decor is primly perfect, the Château de Garrevaques would not be your cup of tea. But if you are looking for a warm welcome, this home truly has heart. Since the 15th century, the Château de Garrevaques has been in the family of the charming Madame Barande who was persuaded by her daughter, Marie-Christine, to open her home as a bed and breakfast. (In fact, the creative Marie-Christine originated the concept of private châteaux in France opening their doors to paying guests.) Although their jobs dictate they must travel, when in town Marie-Christine (a purser for Air France) and Marie-Christine's husband, Claude Combes (a commercial pilot), live at the château. The whole family exudes genuine hospitality. If you have heard the French are aloof, a visit to Château de Garrevaques will quickly dispel that myth—even the cat (Fish) and the dog (Chips) are super friendly. Stay here and become friends with a French family. After a day of sightseeing, there are a swimming pool and tennis court to enjoy in the park. Dinner is a gala event and great fun—filled with tales of the château (ask about the baby born in prison during the revolution who later retrieved his heritage or the faithful gardener who rescued the castle from destruction by the Nazis). *Directions:* From Toulouse take D2/D622 southeast for about 55 km to Revel. Turn northwest on D79 for 5 km to Garrevaques.

CHÂTEAU DE GARREVAQUES
Hosts: Marie-Christine Combes & Andrée Barande
81700 Garrevaques, France
Tel: 05.63.75.04.54, Fax: 05.63.70.26.44
www.karenbrown.com/france/chateaudegarrevaques.html
12 rooms, 8 with private bathrooms; 2 suites share 1 bathroom
Double: 650F Suite (3–5 persons): 1200F
Table d'hôte: 170F per person, includes wine
Open Mar 15 to Dec (groups in winter), Good English spoken
Credit cards: AX, VS
Region: Tarn; Michelin Map 235

It is a short walk through grassy fields to the sea from this wonderful 17th-century manor house. Francois and Agnes Lemarié are a friendly young couple who, along with their four children, enjoy welcoming bed and breakfast guests to their working farm. A strong sense of the past prevails inside the old stone walls of the Lemariés' home and in the adjoining 15th-century chapel converted to a salon for relaxing and listening to music. The past lives on too in the large stone dovecote in the courtyard. This circular dovecote with hundreds of former pigeon niches provides a unique ambiance for guests to enjoy picnics or light meals. Guest bedrooms are basic, and furnishings vary from very simple to family antiques. Dried-flower bouquets warm the somewhat cool stone rooms. Breakfast is served in the Lemariés' dining room reminiscent of days gone by, with its walk-in stone fireplace and hanging copper kettle, heavy beamed ceiling, and old farm furniture. *Directions:* Géfosse is located approximately 30 km northwest of Bayeux. Take N13 west just past Saint Germain du Pert, exit at Osmansville, then take D514 north towards Grandcamp Maisy. Turn left onto D199A to Géfosse. There are roadside signs for several Chambres d'Hôtes so be sure to follow those marked L'Hermerel. It is the second driveway on the right

FERME DE L'HERMEREL (Gîtes de France)
Hosts: Agnes & Francois Lemarié
14230 Géfosse
Fontenay, France
Tel and fax: 02.31.22.64.12
www.karenbrown.com/france/fermedelhermerel.html
4 rooms with private bathrooms
Double: 210F–280F
No table d'hôte
Open all year, Some English spoken
Region: Normandy; Michelin Map 231

The Verjus family's historic farm inn is found in a lovely pastoral setting: on a hill, overlooking green pastures and hills. The only sounds disturbing the rural quiet are cow and sheep bells and a variety of lovely bird songs. The farmhouse is full of historic character, with vaulted ceilings and an old fireplace in the cozy dining room. Built in 1100 and enlarged in the 1700s, the inn combines clean, modern comfort with a traditional ambiance. Home-style dinners usually begin with a regional aperitif called a *macvin*, a potent combination of white wine and whisky, followed by several courses of delicious dishes made with fresh farm ingredients. Guest bedrooms offer good lighting and spotless private showers and WCs. Fresh light-pine furniture and pretty floral-print curtains create an appropriately rustic country atmosphere. *Directions:* Geruge is located approximately 10 km south of Lons le Saunier, capital of the Jura department of France. From Lons, follow designated scenic route D117 through the village of Macornay, and continue up the winding road to Geruge, always following signs for the direction of Saint Julien. Once in Geruge, look for signs directing you to the left for Ferme Auberge La Grange Rouge which is located just outside of the village.

LA GRANGE ROUGE (Gîtes de France)
Hosts: Anne-Marie & Henri Verjus
Geruge
39570 Lons Le Saunier, France
Tel: 03.84.47.00.44, Fax: 03.84.47.34.15
5 rooms with private bathrooms
Double: 230F
Ferme Auberge: 75F per person
Open all year, No English spoken
Region: Jura; Michelin Map 243

When the Konings family (whose home was Holland) asked a realtor to find a place for them to retire to in Provence, they expected the search to take many years. Amazingly, the perfect property, a very old stone farmhouse with great potential charm, was found almost immediately, so, even though the timing was a bit sooner than anticipated, they bought the farmhouse and restored it into an absolute dream. The eight guestrooms, four with air conditioning, are in a cluster of weathered stone buildings which form a small courtyard. The name of each room gives a clue as to its original use such as The Old Kitchen, The Hayloft, and The Wine Press. Arja Konings has exquisite taste and each room is decorated using country antiques and Provençal fabrics. Most conveniently, the Konings' son, Gerald (born in the United States), is a talented chef. He oversees the small restaurant which is delightfully appealing with massive beamed ceiling, tiled floor, exposed stone walls, and country-style antique furnishings. The dining room opens onto a terrace overlooking the swimming pool. Another dining room was added for smokers. *Directions:* Gordes is located about 38 km northeast of Avignon. From Gordes, head east on the D2 for about 2 km. Turn right (south) on D156 and in just a few minutes you will see La Ferme de la Huppe on your right.

LA FERME DE LA HUPPE
Hosts: Arja & Gerald Konings
Route D156
84220 Gordes France
Tel: 04.90.72.12.25, Fax: 04.90.72.01.83
www.karenbrown.com/france/lafermedelahuppe.html
8 rooms with private bathrooms
Double: 450F–700F
No table d'hôte; restaurant (closed Thursdays)
Open Apr to Nov, Fluent English spoken
Credit cards: MC, VS
Region: Provence; Michelin Maps 245, 246

For friends or a large family who are looking for an inexpensive abode while exploring Provence, Les Martins makes a very attractive choice. (It would help if one of your group understands a little French since the Peyrons do not speak English.) The main house where the family lives is a typical old *mas* (farmhouse). The guestrooms are located in an annex found a short stroll up a little lane. Here you will find another characterful building with exposed stone exterior, windows framed with brown shutters, and a roof of heavy tile. The four bedrooms share a pleasant lounge area which is attractively furnished with a large antique wooden table surrounded by country-style chairs. Adding to the rustic ambiance of the room are some antique farm instruments artfully displayed on the walls. Doors open onto a sunny terrace which is shared by all the guests. The bedrooms are basic in decor and ambiance, but for the price, certainly adequate. *Directions:* Gordes is located about 38 km east of Avignon. Although the address is Gordes, Les Martins is actually located much closer to the tiny village of Les Beaumettes, if you can find it on your map. From the N100, take the 103 north towards Gordes. In about 2 km there is a Gîtes de France sign on the left side of the road. Turn left and in a few minutes you will see Les Martins on your left.

LES MARTINS (*Gîtes de France*)
Hosts: Denise & Claude Peyron
84220 Gordes, France
Tel: 04.90.72.24.15, Fax: none
4 rooms with private showers
Double: 260F
Table d'hôte: 100F per person
Open Feb to Nov 15, No English spoken
Region: Provence; Michelin Maps 245, 246

The Moulin de Fresquet is truly a jewel, offering not only the charm of an old mill, but also beautiful antiques and great warmth of welcome. The hearth of the old stone mill dates back to the 17th century. The mill stream still flows right beneath the house—in fact, from Room 4 (Bief), you can look out the casement windows and watch and listen to the gurgling waters. Many places to stay in this price range are pleasant, but lacking in style: not so with Moulin de Fresquet. The family room where guests gather for dinner is filled with beautiful antiques that Gérard inherited from his grandmother. The ambiance is one of rustic beauty with handsome stone walls accented by family portraits and 200-year-old tapestries, heavy beamed ceiling, bouquets of fresh flowers, and a massive stone fireplace. A narrow staircase leads to the attractive bedrooms which have color-coordinated draperies and bedspreads and french doors which open onto private patios. Claude, so pretty with sparkling brown eyes, is a wonderful cook and dinner must not be missed. This pleasing old mill is conveniently located for visiting the fascinating town of Rocamadour. *Directions:* From Gramat take N140 south towards Figeac. Just 500 meters after leaving Gramat, take the small lane on the left signposted to Moulin de Fresquet—the mill is on your right.

MOULIN DE FRESQUET (Gîtes de France)
Hosts: Claude & Gérard Ramelot
46500 Gramat, France
Tel and fax: 05.65.38.70.60, Car: 06.08.85.09.21
www.karenbrown.com/france/moulindefresquet.html
6 rooms with private bathrooms
Double: 270F–390F
Table d'hôte: 110F per person, includes wine
Open Apr to Nov, Some English spoken
Region: Dordogne; Michelin Maps 235, 239

If you are looking for a tranquil little hideaway while exploring the beautiful area of Provence, the Domaine du Bois Vert is truly a gem. Although the construction is only a few years old, the clever owners, Jean Peter and Véronique Richard, have tastefully achieved the ambiance of an old farmhouse by incorporating a typical rosy-tan stuccoed exterior, light-blue wooden shutters, and a heavy tiled roof. The mood of antiquity continues within where dark beamed ceilings, tiled floors, dark wooden doors, and white walls enhance a few carefully chosen country-style Provençal pieces of furniture and country print fabrics. There are three bedrooms, each immaculately tidy and prettily decorated. The bedroom to the back of the house is especially enticing, with windows looking out onto the oak trees. Meals are not served on a regular basis, but Véronique treats guests who stay a week to a dinner featuring typical regional specialties. The swimming pool is a most refreshing bonus. *Directions:* Grans is approximately 40 km southeast of Arles and 6 km from Salon de Provence. From Grans, go south on D19 (signposted to Lançon-Provence). About 1 km after you pass Grans, turn left on a small road where you will see a Gîtes sign. In a few minutes turn left again at another Gîtes sign and take the lane to the Domaine du Bois Vert.

DOMAINE DU BOIS VERT (Gîtes de France)
Hosts: Véronique & Jean Peter Richard
Quartier Montauban
13450 Grans, France
Tel and fax: 04.90.55.82.98
www.karenbrown.com/france/domaineduboisvert.html
3 rooms with private bathrooms
Double: 290F–320F
No table d'hôte
Open all year, Good English spoken
Region: Provence; Michelin Maps 245, 246

Jacqueline and Auguste Bahuaud purchased a handsome manor dating from the mid-1800s and, with great love and labor, meticulously restored the house to its original splendor. Throughout the home everything is fresh, new, and beautifully decorated. The bedrooms are especially outstanding: each has its own personality, each is very inviting. My particular favorite is the blue room which has a prime corner location, affording windows on two walls looking out to the rear garden. One of the very nicest aspects of Chez Bahuaud is its setting: the parklike grounds stretch behind the house with terraced lawns shaded by mature trees. A romantic path through the garden leads down to Grez-Neuville, a real gem of a small village nestled on the banks of the Mayenne river. There are many boats along the Mayenne that can be rented by the day or week for exploring the picturesque countryside. Your gracious hosts, Jacqueline and Auguste, warmly open their home and hearts to their guests. *Directions:* From Angers, take N162 north for about 17 km and take a right on to the Grez-Neuville exit. Go into the village and find the old church. As you go down towards the river, you see on your left a beautiful old stone church, and just adjacent to it, the Chambres d'Hôtes sign on the gate of the Bahuauds' home.

LA CROIX D'ETAIN (Gîtes de France)
Hosts: Jacqueline & Auge Bahuaud
2, Rue de l'Ecluse
49220 Grez-Neuville, France
Tel: 02.41.95.68.49, Fax: 02.41.18.02.72
www.karenbrown.com/france/lacroixdetain.html
4 rooms with private bathrooms
Double: 360F–390F
No table d'hôte
Open all year, Some English spoken
Region: Loire Valley; Michelin Map 232

During Brigitte Godon's frequent visits to the Saint Tropez area, she had often admired Le Mazet des Mûres, a lovely 19th-century villa, so when the property came up for sale, she and her husband quickly decided to buy it. The timing was superb as Jean Pierre had retired as a movie director and Brigitte was ready to slow down her career as a movie editor. They renovated the house and restored the gardens and what you see today is a charming villa whose pink façade is laced with vines and accented by violet-colored shutters. A front gate leads into a courtyard shaded by an ancient gnarled oak tree and beautified by colorful flowers. In this secluded courtyard white tables and chairs are set for breakfast and the evening meal (reservations required). Each bedroom, although not large, enjoys a kitchenette where guests can fix themselves a light meal. My favorite (number 2) is a corner room with a double bed with antique wrought-iron headboard and pretty yellow Provençal-print curtains and bedspread. Guests at Le Mazet des Mûres can enjoy utter tranquillity where only the chirping of the cicadas disturbs the quiet—yet be just minutes from the frenzy of the Côte d'Azur's beach resorts. *Directions:* Take RN98 from Saint Maxime towards Saint Tropez. After 4 km turn right at the roundabout, towards Parc de Grimaud Pierres and Vacances. Go about 1 km and turn right on a tiny lane signposted Le Mazet des Mûres.

LE MAZET DES MÛRES
Hosts: Brigitte & Jean Pierre Decourt
Route du Cros d'Entassi
83310 Grimaud, France
Tel & fax: 04.94.56.44.45
www.karenbrown.com/france/lemazetdesmures.html
5 rooms with private bathrooms
Double: 400F
Table d'hôte: 100F per person, includes wine
Open Easter to mid-Oct, Very good English spoken
Region: Côte d'Azur; Michelin Map 245

La Roseraie, a pretty buff-colored house enhanced by white shutters and a steeply pitched tile roof with jaunty gables, is owned by an English couple, Roz and John Binns. John is still engaged as an airline pilot but Roz, who was previously an airline stewardess, now devotes full time to caring for her guests. She is a natural for the task—her exuberant charm and natural warmth are sure to win your heart. The Binns bought La Roseraie in a sadly neglected state, which gave them the opportunity during the renovations to add four bedrooms with private bathrooms for guests. Roz decorated each of them with a similar motif, using pretty English country-floral fabrics at the windows and again on the draperies that are gathered into a coronet above beds. My favorite, number 8, is tucked up under the eaves with exposed rafters and gabled windows through which the sun streams into the room. La Roseraie has a distinct English-style bed and breakfast informality. Although the bedrooms are neat and tidy, the rest of the home has a very informal, lived-in look to it—just as if you came to stay as a guest in a private home. *Directions:* Exit the A6 at Mâcon Sud and take the N79 to Cluny, and then the D980 towards Montceau les Mines for 21 km. Turn left on the D983 towards Saint Bonnet de Joux (8.5 km), and right on the D27 to La Guiche. At the town square turn left beside the town hall—the bed and breakfast is on your right.

LA ROSERAIE (Gîtes de France)
Hosts: Roz & John Binns
71220 La Guiche, France
Tel: 03.85.24.67.82, Fax: 03.85.24.61.03
www.karenbrown.com/france/laroseraie.html
4 rooms with private bathrooms
Double: 410F
No table d'hôte
Open all year, Fluent English spoken
Region: Burgundy; Michelin Map 243

A romantic, enchanted quality pervades the lovely old Moulin de la Dive, a former flour mill covered with ivy and surrounded by magical wooded grounds. Originally built by a noble family in the 14th century, the mill was burned by the Protestants in 1569 and rebuilt in the early 17th century, only to be burned again during the French Revolution. Annick Vanverts and her husband are extremely warm and solicitous hosts who relocated here from Paris, seeking a more natural existence away from the fast pace and pollution of the big city. Guests have a private entrance through an old arched doorway and up a marble staircase to the two bedrooms, each uniquely decorated. Seville is furnished entirely in Spanish antiques, while Nohant reflects the graceful style of 18th-century France and is named after the home of novelist Georges Sand. The rooms have spotless, modern bathrooms and large windows which let in the pure country air. Breakfast is enjoyed either in the Vanverts' charming, country-elegant salon or outside in the lush garden. *Directions:* Guron is located approximately 30 km southwest of Poitiers. Take N10 in the direction of Angoulême for about 28 km then go in the direction Payré (on the right). After the second traffic circle, head for Voulon-Guron. After 2 km, look for a Chambres d'Hôtes sign marking the Vanverts' gate on the right.

LE MOULIN DE LA DIVE
Hosts: Monsieur & Madame Vanverts
Guron, 86700 Payré, France
Tel: 05.49.42.40.97, Fax: none
2 rooms with private bathrooms
Double: 360F–380F
No table d'hôte
Open Jul & Aug, Very little English spoken
Region: Atlantic Coast; Michelin Map 233

Dana and Robert Ornsteen, your charming American hosts, lived for many years in Paris before purchasing L'Enclos, an enchanting hamlet in the heart of the idyllic Périgord. The complex (once the domain of the Count de Souffron) forms a courtyard. On one side is the manor, a soft-beige, two-story home, prettily accented by white shutters. Also facing the courtyard is a cluster of stone cottages which exude charm and a whimsical, story-book character with their jumble of steep, weathered, interconnecting roof-lines and perky gables. Two guestrooms are found in the manor house—the others occupy the hamlet's ivy-laced, yellow-hued stone cottages. The cottages are named for their "past": La Boulangerie still has its bread ovens, La Chapelle occupies the old church, romantic Rose Cottage (one of my favorites) has thick stone walls, painted furniture, and Provençal fabrics. Two cottages have full kitchens. The gardens are outstanding, with immaculately tended lawns terraced by stone walls and studded with gorgeous flowerbeds. A swimming pool nestles in a lush grassy oasis. Everything is perfection and the price is incredible for such quality. *Directions:* From Périgueux take D5 east towards Hautefort. At Tourtoirac turn left, cross the bridge, keep right at the Y, and continue for 1.4 km. Turn left into the lane signposted Pragelier, go down the hill and through the gates to L'Enclos.

L'ENCLOS
Hosts: Dana & Robert Ornsteen
Pragelier, 24390 Hautefort, France
Tel: 05.53.51.11.40, Fax: 05.53 50 37 21
Tel: 52.415.21337, Fax: 52.415.27135 (Mexico–Nov to Apr 15)
www.karenbrown.com/france/lenclos.html
2 rooms, 9 cottages, with private bathrooms, 2 night min.
Double: 350F–750F
Table d'hôte: 125F per person, includes wine*
*Wednesdays only Jul & Aug
Open May to Oct 15, Fluent English spoken, No children under 13
Region: Périgord; Michelin Map 233

In the lovely Périgord region of France, tucked along the banks of a small river, you find the quaint Le Moulin de la Crouzille. This story-book-perfect, vine-covered old mill abounds with character: it is constructed of mellow-toned, honey-colored stone highlighted by casement windows and pretty white shutters. The steeply pitched roof (a jumble of interesting angles) appears even more whimsical with perky little dormer windows peeking out. Stone steps lead up to the front door which opens directly into a homey living room where comfortable chairs and a sofa are grouped around a large open fireplace. To the left of the fireplace, a door opens to a terrace where dinner is served in the summer. There are two bedrooms, each with its own bathroom down the hall. Our favorite is the bedroom with the wonderful painted four-poster bed. The owners, Diana and John Armitage, born in England, now make France their home. Guests are welcomed as friends and dine with the family—Diana is a superb cook and personally prepares the meals. As an added bonus, guests enjoy a swimming pool within a walled garden. *Directions*: From Périgueux take D5 east towards Hautefort. Two and a half km after passing through the village of Tourtoirac, turn left at a small crossroads signposted La Palue and La Crouzille. Turn right at the first lane, crossing a small bridge to Le Moulin de la Crouzille (30 km east of Périgueux).

LE MOULIN DE LA CROUZILLE
Hosts: Diana & John Armitage
Tourtoirac
24390 Hautefort, France
Tel & fax: 05.53.51.11.94
E-mail: wolsey@wolseylo.demon.co.uk
2 rooms with private bathrooms
Double: 700 F
Table d'hôte: 200F per person
Closed Christmas, Fluent English spoken
Region: Périgord; Michelin Map 233

The old manor house of Le Petit Pey is set in pretty grounds and tended with care by energetic hostess Annie de Bosredon, a very charming, refined, yet down-to-earth hostess who takes great pleasure in opening her home to guests. Le Petit Pey is a regional stone building with windows and French doors framed by white shutters. The oldest part dates from the 1600s, while the newer wing was added in about 1760. Madame de Bosredon's aristocratic drawing room combines comfort with elegance and is filled with valuable antiques, artifacts, and fresh-cut garden roses. Bedrooms are furnished in family antiques, and each has its own country charm. The drawing room and bedrooms are actually in a separate wing of the house, so guests are afforded privacy and the luxury of being at home in the lovely salon. There are plenty of historic walled towns in the region as well as the interesting towns of Issigeac and Bergerac. *Directions:* Issigeac is approximately 60 km south of Périgueux via 21 through Bergerac. About 11 km after Bergerac, turn left onto D14 towards Issigeac, then at Issigeac take D21 south towards Castillonnes. Two km later at Monmarvès, look for a sign reading Domaine du Petit Pey and turn into the green gate.

LE PETIT PEY (Gîtes de France)
Hostess: Annie de Bosredon
Monmarvès
24560 Issigeac, France
Tel: 05.53.58.70.61, Fax: none
www.karenbrown.com/france/lepetitpey.html
2 rooms with private bathrooms
Double: 380F
No table d'hôte
Open Apr to Oct15, Good English spoken
Region: Périgord; Michelin Map 235

The Château du Plessis is a lovely, aristocratic country home, truly one of France's most exceptional private châteaux and a personal favorite. Madame Benoist's family has lived here since well before the revolution, but the antiques throughout the home are later acquisitions of her great-great-great-grandfather, as the furnishings original to the house were burned on the front lawn by the revolutionaries in 1793. Furnishings throughout the home are elegant, yet the Benoists establish an atmosphere of homey comfort. Artistic fresh-flower arrangements abound and one can see Madame's cutting garden from the French doors in the salon which open onto the lush grounds. In the evening the large oval table in the dining room provides an opportunity to enjoy the company of other guests and the country-fresh cuisine of Madame Benoist. The Benoists are a handsome couple who take great pride in their home and the welcome they extend to their guests. *Directions:* To reach La Jaille-Yvon travel north of Angers on N162 and at the town of Le Lion d'Angers clock the odometer 11 km farther north to an intersection, Carrefour Fleur de Lys. Turn east and travel 2½ km to La Jaille-Yvon—the Château du Plessis is on its southern edge.

CHÂTEAU DU PLESSIS
Hosts: Simone & Paul Benoist
49990 La Jaille-Yvon, France
Tel: 02.41.95.12.75, Fax: 02.41.95.14.41
www.karenbrown.com/france/chateauduplessis.html
8 rooms with private bathrooms
Double: 600F–850F
Table d'hôte: 270F per person
Open Apr to Nov, Very good English spoken
Credit cards: all major
Region: Loire Valley; Michelin Map 232

Christel Hofstadt came to Provence on a holiday from Germany and fell in love with the absolute tranquillity surrounding the Mas Soupétrière. Although the stone farmhouse was in complete disrepair, she could not resist buying it. The home has been completely renovated and is now open as a delightful bed and breakfast. The façade of the house is very attractive: a combination of honey-colored stone interspersed with light-tan stuccoed walls, heavy tiled roof, and light-gray-blue shutters. Christel has excellent taste and the decor is fresh and pretty, with country antiques, Provençal-style fabrics, white plastered walls, and Oriental carpets. Meals are usually served outside on a pretty terrace in front of the house (a hearty dinner, featuring the specialties of Provence and wine, is included in the room rate). An added bonus is the swimming pool located in a field near the house. Christel requests that, if possible, guests stay for more than two days. *Directions:* Gordes is located 38 km northeast of Avignon. From N100, take D60 north towards Joucas. Before Joucas, turn right (east) on the D2. Turn left at the second road (marked D102) and take the very first lane to your right. In a few minutes you will see the bed and breakfast on your left.

MAS DE LA SOUPÉTRIÈRE (Gîtes de France)
Hostess: Christel Hofstadt
Joucas
84220 Gordes, France
Tel: 04.90.05.78.81, Fax: 04.90.05.76.33
2 rooms with private bathrooms
Double: 900F, includes breakfast & dinner
Table d'hôte included in room rate
Open Mar to Nov, Fluent English spoken
Region: Provence; Michelin Maps 245, 246

Judy (who is English) and Jan (who is Dutch) bought the Mas du Bas Claux just outside the charming medieval village of Lacoste when Jan took early retirement from the Dupont Company. It took several years of dedicated labor, but what had been a neglected 18th-century stone farmhouse is now a stunning home and an outstanding bed and breakfast. Jan is a keen gardener and, when the house was redesigned, the setting was also restructured so that what was previously a steeply sloping field is now a flat, beautifully manicured lawn enhanced with flowerbeds. From this lush terrace there is a romantic outlook over the vineyards and beyond to the beckoning hills. Also in the garden there is a large, beautifully designed swimming pool, a lovely place to relax after a day of sightseeing. It is not the beauty of the house or garden, however, that makes this place so perfect: it is the warmth of the owners, Judy and Jan who are perfect hosts. They are not listed in any of the official bed and breakfast organizations because they wish to remain small and exclusive, maintaining the size and quality to treat each and everyone as a friend and pampered guest. *Directions:* Lacoste is located 45 km east of Avignon. Take the D108 east from Lacoste. After 2 km, watch for a sign on the left side of the road for Mas du Bas Claux.

MAS DU BAS CLAUX
Hosts: Judy & Jan van Horck
84480 Lacoste, France
Tel: 04.90.75.90.49, Fax: 04.90.75.96.17
www.karenbrown.com/france/masdubasclaux.html
2 rooms with private bathrooms
Double: 550F, 500F for 7 or more nights
3-night minimum stay
No table d'hôte
Closed Jul and Aug, tel & fax when closed: 04.50.34.14.82
Fluent English spoken
Region: Provence; Michelin Maps 245, 246

The enchanting Château du Guilguiffin is a gorgeous stone manor accented by white shutters, steeply pitched slate roof, perky dormers, and a profusion of chimneys. A circular drive sweeps to the entrance which faces onto a lawn enclosed by a circular wall interrupted by 18th-century columns with unique Oriental motifs which make this 1100-acre property a "historic site." The elegant décor is outstanding with beamed-ceilings, mellow wood paneling, and heirloom antiques. In contrast to the formal parlor, the breakfast room is delightfully casual—a happy room with pretty yellow walls, blue doors, blue-and-white tiles, and a "walk-in" stone fireplace. Guests enjoy breakfast at one large table topped by a gay Provençal-print cloth. The bedrooms are exquisitely furnished with antiques accented by fabric-covered walls and color-coordinating draperies and bedspreads. The garden too is equally stunning. Early spring presents an unbelievable spectacle of 400,000 daffodils followed by thousands of azaleas and rhododendrons. Barbecues are available so guests can grill fresh fish from the local market and enjoy dinner in the parklike grounds. But what makes a stay here truly special is the genuine hospitality of your host, Philippe Davy (the château has been handed down in his family for over 900 years). Stay at least a week to explore the best of Brittany. *Directions:* From Quimper, west on D784 direction Audierne. The Château is on the left, 3 km before Landudec.

CHÂTEAU DU GUILGUIFFIN
Host: Philippe Davy
Guilguiffin, 29710 Landudec, France
Tel: 02.98.91.52.11, Fax: 02.98.91.52.52
www.karenbrown.com/france/chateauduguilguiffin.html
6 rooms with private bathrooms
Double: 650F–800F, suites 1100–1300F (3–4 persons)
No table d'hôte, barbecue in garden, 10-minutes to restaurants
Open Apr to Oct 12, by reservation only, Fluent English spoken
Credit cards: AX, VS
Region: Brittany; Michelin Map 230

Le Bas du Gast is not in the countryside, but is rather a country estate within a city. Once through the massive green wooden gates, you enter a fantasy land of sculpted hedges, wooded parkland, paths leading to English-style gardens, fish ponds, and secluded nooks for dreaming. The years slip away and you feel as if you are living once again in the 18th century. There is an authenticity to this château that is rarely found. During the renovation, there was great integrity in preserving the original character of the building. Your gracious host, François Williot (who has the manner and speech of an English lord of the manor), loves his home and can point out to you the perfect symmetry of the formal gardens whose design dates back many centuries, as well as many of the fine architectural features of the house which you might otherwise miss. The furnishings within the home include stunning family heirlooms from the time of Louis XV. Although formality and grandeur prevail in the furnishings, there is also the comfortable, lived-in ambiance of a family home. There is not a hint of stiff formality in your welcome—you are made to feel like a guest of the family. *Directions:* Follow signs to Centre Ville, then Salle Polyvalente. The château is directly across the street from the Bibliothèque which is adjacent to the well-marked Salle Polyvalente.

LE BAS DU GAST
Hosts: Monsieur & Madame François Charles Williot
6, Rue de la Halle aux Toiles
53000 Laval, France
Tel: 02.43.49.22.79, Fax: 02.43.56.44.71
www.karenbrown.com/france/lebasdugast.html
5 rooms with private bathrooms
Double: 770F–870F Suite: 1,320F
No table d'hôte, Children welcome
Open Feb to Nov, Fluent English spoken
Credit cards: AX
Region: Loire Valley; Michelin Map 232

If you want to experience a stay in a typical French farmhouse, Montpeyroux, a handsome, large two-story home, softened by ivy and white shutters, makes an excellent choice. The ambiance within does not conform to any trendy decorating scheme—this is truly a family home with old-fashioned furnishings. However, I was quite impressed: the bedrooms are all wallpapered and have color-coordinated draperies, cushions, and bedspreads—all beautifully sewn by Madame Sallier. Splurge and request the most expensive room—not only because it is the largest, but also because it is just beautiful, with genuine antiques set off by a color scheme of creams and greens. The farm also has its own swimming pool and tennis court—quite a surprise for such a simple farmhouse. *Directions:* Castres is located 71 km east of Toulouse. From Castres go southwest on N126 then D622 towards Revel. About 18 km after leaving Castres turn north on D12 to Lempaut and from Lempaut drive west on D46 for about 2 km. When you come to a large cemetery on your left, turn left on the small road just before it—the road loops around the cemetery. Follow this road until you see the Gîtes sign and the large home on your right.

MONTPEYROUX
Hosts: Monsieur & Madame Sallier
Montpeyroux
81700 Lempaut, France
Tel & fax: 05.63.75.51.17
www.karenbrown.com/france/montpeyroux.html
5 rooms, 3 with private bathrooms
Double: 250F–300F
Table d'hôte: 100F per person
Open Apr to Nov, No English spoken
Region: Tarn; Michelin Map 235

A stay at the lovely Château de Longecourt is a wonderful opportunity to experience life in a French country castle. Surrounded on all sides by a tranquil moat, the castle has a delicate fairy-tale quality enhanced by its graceful towers and neo-classical Italian decoration. Inside, the elegant, gilt-trimmed salon, dining room, reception rooms, and library are all furnished and decorated in authentic antiques from the Louis XV period. Bedrooms are also highly charming generously furnished with beautiful antiques, Oriental rugs, paintings, and objets d'art. Each room is unique, with intimate tower bedrooms featuring stone vaulted ceilings and others offering marble fireplaces and tall windows overlooking the peaceful grounds. The Château de Longecourt is as memorable for its exquisite surroundings as for the warm welcome extended by the Comtesse de Saint-Seine and her personable sons. They make an effort to pamper their guests with luxurious details such as bedtime chocolates and copious breakfasts served on heirloom china. *Directions:* Longecourt en Plaine is located approximately 15 km southeast of Dijon, on the Burgundy canal. Leave Dijon on D968 following signs for Longecourt en Plaine. Once in the village, signs for Château de Longecourt point the way to the castle which is located near the church.

CHÂTEAU DE LONGECOURT
Hostess: Comtesse de Saint-Seine
Longecourt en Plaine
21110 Genlis, France
Tel: 03.80.39.88.76, Fax: 03.80.39.87.44
www.karenbrown.com/france/chateaudelongecourt.html
4 rooms with private bathrooms
Double: 700F Suite: 700F–1,000F
Table d'hôte: 250F
Open all year, Some English spoken
Region: Burgundy; Michelin Map 243

From the moment you drive through the gates, you will be enchanted by the Manoir Saint-Gilles, a story-book perfect, 15th-century château accented by manicured lawns, clipped box hedges, and fragrant rose gardens. It is immediately obvious that the owners are perfectionists for everything is tended immaculately. One wing of the house, a charming two-story stone building accented by a tall turret, is totally dedicated to guests. It has an inviting lounge where small tables with colorful Provençal tablecloths are set in front of a massive stone fireplace. The attractively decorated bedrooms are reached by the stone staircase which spirals up the tower. My favorite is room 3, an exceptionally large room with windows capturing a view of the front garden and the wooded park behind. Your gracious hosts, Monsieur and Madame Naux, have a daughter married to an American, and they seem especially to enjoy entertaining guests from abroad. *Directions:* Coming from Angers on the RN147, take D53 marked to Blou and Saint Philbert. Very soon after leaving the highway, D53 goes over the railroad tracks which are hard to see as they cross beneath the road in a low gully. At the first road after crossing the tracks, turn left and then turn left again at the first road. Go about 300 meters and take the first small lane on your right (there is no sign but you will see the château on your right).

MANOIR SAINT-GILLES (Gîtes de France)
Hosts: Monsieur & Madame Naux
49160 Longué, France
Tel: 02.41.38.77.45, Fax: 02.41.52.67.82
www.karenbrown.com/france/manoirsaintgilles.html
4 rooms with private bathrooms
Double: 340F–380F
No table d'hôte
Open Apr to Nov, No English spoken
Region: Loire Valley; Michelin Map 232

Three hundred meters from Brittany's northern coastline, Madame Sillard's historic home is the former residence of author Ernest Renan. Set in wooded grounds, this small manor house is furnished in lovely country antiques and offers bed and breakfast accommodation to fortunate travelers. A lace-curtained front door leads into the entry hall which is warmly decorated with an antique armoire, bookcase, and dried-flower arrangements. Madame Sillard is a charming, well-traveled hostess who has spent extended periods of time in the United States, thus speaks very good English. Her guest bedrooms are decorated with pretty fabrics and fresh-flower bouquets, while furnishings are a tasteful mix of antiques and some more contemporary pieces. Breakfast is served at a long wooden table in the country-elegant drawing room where two tabby cats often share the seat of a tapestry chair. *Directions:* Louannec is located approximately 70 km northwest of Saint Brieuc, 40 km northwest of Guingamp. From Lannion (30 km northwest of Guingamp), take D788 north in the direction of Perros Guirec. After 7 km, turn right onto D6 to Louannec. Just before town, there will be a sign indicating Chambres d'Hôtes up a small lane to the right. A driveway on the left leads to Madame's pretty house set back behind a garden.

DEMEURE DE ROSMAPAMON
Hostess: Madame A. Sillard
Louannec
22700 Perros-Guirec, France
Tel: 02.96.23.00.87, Fax: none
www.karenbrown.com/france/demeurederosmapamon.html
5 rooms, 2 with private bathrooms
Double: 375F Suite: 410F
No table d'hôte
Open Apr to Oct, Very good English spoken
Credit cards: VS
Region: Brittany; Michelin Map 230

Michel Descorps resides in a long, low country house reminiscent of stable buildings. He did indeed once keep a full stable of horses here and is a former champion of the French four-in-hand competition. Inside, his ivy-covered ranch-style home has a very British country-cottage feeling: in fact, Monsieur avows himself to be quite an Anglophile. Laura Ashley wallpapers such as the pretty, yet understated, Scottish thistle patterns decorate the walls in his guest bedrooms, while Cecil Aldin prints brighten the hallways. Bathrooms are all newly renovated and extremely clean, modern, and well equipped. All the accommodations are fresh and very tasteful, with rustic antique furniture and old exposed support beams adding historic character to the rooms. Table d'hôte dinners are available with advance notice and are served in the cozy dining room full of Cecil Aldin prints on a background of green-striped wallpaper. In the morning, guests are pampered with breakfast in their rooms, on the terrace, or in a small room opening off the garden. Note: The Château of Luynes is now open to the public. *Directions:* Luynes is located approximately 10 km west of Tours on the north bank of the Loire. Le Quart is not in Luynes, but north of town in the countryside. Take N152 from Tours to Luynes, then turn north onto D49 towards Pernay. Continue towards Pernay on D6 and at Le Maupas take the first right turn, after which the first driveway on the right is signposted Le Quart.

LE QUART
Hosts: Monsieur & Madame Michel Descorps
37230 Luynes, France
Tel: 02.47.55.51.70, Fax: 02.47.55.57.49
4 rooms with private bathrooms
Double: 550F–950F
Table d'hôte: price varies
Open all year, Fluent English spoken
Region: Loire Valley; Michelin Map 232

The Marcs are friendly country folk who have lived in their ivy-covered former stable house for over 20 years while converting it, bit by bit, to the comfortable, if modest, home it is today. This is a working farm, where the Marcs raise cattle, sheep, chickens, and the occasional goose. Their home is very clean and well kept. They offer three guestrooms in the main house and an apartment just across the pretty courtyard. The bedrooms are furnished simply but with taste—antique-style pieces decorate every room, all of which have private baths. The Marcs have made every effort to make their home comfortable and welcoming for guests and are ready to help in any way. Although the Marcs speak very little English, they overcome any language barriers with their warm welcome and farm-style hospitality. *Directions:* Mainneville is located about 75 km northwest of Paris via A15 to Pontoise, then D915 through Gisors, and finally on D14 to Mainneville. In Mainneville, look for a green-and-yellow Chambres d'Hôtes sign directing you to the Marcs' farm. Located just on the edge of town, the low, ivy-covered house is set back from the road with a lush green lawn and big trees in front. Pretty natural-wood shutters flank all the doors and windows.

FERME DE SAINTE GENEVIÈVE (Gîtes de France)
Hosts: Jeannine & Jean-Claude Marc
27150 Mainneville, France
Tel: 02.32.55.51.26, Fax: 02.32.27.50.89
www.karenbrown.com/france/fermedesaintegenevieve.html
4 rooms with private bathrooms
Double: from 220F
No table d'hôte
Open all year, Very little English spoken
Region: Normandy; Michelin Map 237

In its prime, the Château Unang was undoubtedly one of the showplaces of Provence. Today the formal gardens show a genteel neglect and the gorgeous château reflects a faded elegance, but the fairy-tale quality of this 18th-century château remains undimmed. Iron gates open to the inner courtyard, overlooked by the handsome beige-stucco château whose exterior is softened by ivy and whose windows are accented by white wooden shutters. The château fronts onto a gravel terrace with steps leading down to a lower terrace with a garden of clipped hedges forming an intricate design. More steps go down to an even lower level where the vineyards hug the edge of an idyllically positioned swimming pool. The guestrooms are found up a flight of stone steps from the reception hall. Furnished with antiques, the bedrooms are decorated in a homey, comfortable style. My favorite room, Marquessa, has a splendid view of the vineyards. Marie Lefer is your gracious young hostess—Château Unang is her family home. She is in charge of the bed and breakfast while her brother oversees the vineyards and production of the family's wines. *Directions:* From the A7 (Orange to Aix en Provence) take the Avignon North exit. Follow signs to Carpentras then take D4 for 6 km towards Venasque, turning left on D5 to Malemort du Comtat. From Malemort take D5 towards Méthamis. After 1 km there is a small sign on the right leading to Château Unang.

CHÂTEAU UNANG (Gîtes de France)
Hostess: Marie Lefer
84570 Malemort, France
Tel: 04.90.69.71.06, Fax: 04.90.69.92.80
www.karenbrown.com/france/chateauunang.html
4 rooms with private bathrooms
Double: 600F–700F Suite (Jul & Aug only): 950F
Table d'hôte: 180F per person, includes wine
Open all year, Good English spoken
Credit cards: VS, MC
Region: Provence; Michelin Map 245

A real find, the Loisels' Georgian-style farmhouse is tastefully furnished with family antiques and pleasing color combinations. The high-ceilinged guest bedrooms are decorated with pretty flower-print wallpapers, complemented by carpets and upholstery in soft color tones. Bathrooms are scrupulously clean and well equipped. Downstairs in her dining room furnished in country antiques, Madame Loisel serves delicious breakfasts and table d'hôte dinners featuring fresh farm produce. The imposing oak armoire and sideboard date from the time of her grandparents' marriage and add to the peaceful feeling of history and continuity that pervades Madame Loisel's lovely home. This pleasant bed and breakfast is enhanced by your energetic hostess who enjoys introducing her guests to regional dinner specialties and also teaches lace making and embroidery. *Directions:* Manneville la Goupil is located about 26 km northeast of Le Havre via N15 to Saint Romain de Coulbosc, then D10 to Manneville la Goupil. Across from the church you see a green-and-yellow Chambres d'Hôtes sign that directs you to turn left onto a small road leading out of town. About 1.5 km later, turn right at the white fence that has a Gîtes de France sign posted on it.

FERME DE L'ÉCOSSE (Gîtes de France)
Hosts: Nicole & Hubert Loisel
Manneville La Goupil
76110 Goderville, France
Tel and fax: 02.35.27.77.21
4 rooms, 3 with private bathrooms
Double: 250F–280F
Table d'hôte: 125F, includes cider
Open Feb to Dec 15, No English spoken
Region: Normandy; Michelin Map 231

The 19th-century Château de la Fredière, on the hillside overlooking the surrounding farmland and the village of Céron, is a pretty cream-colored stone château with delicate end turrets and a silvery-gray slate roof. The size of the room and whether or not it has a private bathroom determines the price. Madame Charlier is a charming and attentive hostess. Her son maintains the castle's 18-hole golf course and her daughter-in-law oversees the restaurant. (Dinners are on a reservation-only basis.) A bountiful Continental breakfast is served in the dining room before the fireplace, at an intimate table set in the turret, or, on pretty days, in the morning sun on the terrace. Not luxurious, the Château de la Fredière instead offers comfortable, reasonably priced accommodations and a friendly welcome. *Directions:* From Lyon take the N7 west to Roanne. From Roanne go north on D482 for 71 km to Marcigny. At Marcigny go west on the D990 to Urbisse, then north to Céron.

CHÂTEAU DE LA FREDIÈRE
Hostess: Edith Charlier
Céron
71110 Marcigny, France
Tel: 03.85.25.19.67, Fax: 03.85.25.35.01
9 rooms, 2 suites, with private bathrooms
Double: 310F–730F Suite: 860F
No table d'hôte; restaurant at golf club
Open Mar 15 to Nov 15, Fluent English spoken
Credit cards: MC, VS
Region: Burgundy; Michelin Map 238

We received a warm welcome at Monsieur and Madame Bouteillers' charming half-timbered farmhouse where they have made their home for over 40 years. Monsieur explained that he was originally a city boy from Rouen, but always wanted to be a farmer. He has achieved his dream in this pastoral setting where he and his wife have raised seven children. Madame's table d'hôte dinners always include regional specialties such as creamed chicken, duck with peach sauce, and, of course, one of several varieties of homemade apple tarts. These friendly meals are served in the light and cheerful entry salon with its long table decorated with a wildflower bouquet in an earthenware jug. An antique sideboard and old stone mantel displaying pewter candlesticks add to the country ambiance. The Bouteillers' two guestrooms are clean and well equipped with simple decor and furnishings, including wooden beds and armoires. *Directions:* Martainville is located approximately 58 km southwest from Rouen via A13 to the Beuzeville exit. In Beuzeville, turn left at the traffic light at the church. Follow signs for the town of Epaignes via route D27. Approximately 6 km later you see a Chambres d'Hôtes sign directing you to turn right. A driveway on the left then leads you to the Bouteillers' low, half-timbered farmhouse.

CHEZ BOUTEILLER (Gîtes de France)
Hosts: Monsieur & Madame Jacques Bouteiller
Martainville
27210 Beuzeville, France
Tel: 02.32.57.82.23, Fax: none
2 rooms with private bathrooms
Double: 210F
Table d'hôte: 90F per person
Open all year, Some English spoken by Monsieur
Region: Normandy; Michelin Map 231

The small, out-of-the-way village of Maureilhan is for travelers who like to get off the beaten track. A stay at the Fabre-Barthezs' simple, but comfortable home is a convivial, relaxing experience, a refreshing change from the impersonal atmosphere of many hotels. Monsieur and Madame are friendly wine growers who produce rosé and red wines in addition to welcoming bed and breakfast guests. They enjoy beginning an evening with a shared house aperitif, followed by a delicious four-course table d'hôte dinner, and perhaps completed by a group sing-along. Meals are most often enjoyed in the small, tree-shaded garden where Madame grills savory meats over grapevine branches. Peaceful bedrooms are located upstairs and are accessible through French doors from an outdoor balcony overlooking the courtyard and garden. Furnishings and decor are homelike and comfortable, with touches such as brass beds, crocheted coverlets, and embroidered tablecloths. *Directions:* Exit the A7 (Montpellier to Narbonne) at Béziers. Take N112 northwest in the direction of Saint Pons until reaching the village of Maureilhan. Once in the village, follow Chambres d'Hôtes signs to the second right, then right again under a stone archway to the courtyard of Les Arbousiers.

LES ARBOUSIERS (Gîtes de France)
Hosts: Marie Andrée & Léon Fabre-Barthez
7, Rue Jean Jaures
Maureilhan
34310 Cazouls Les Béziers, France
Tel: 04.67.90.52.49, Fax: 04.67.90.50.50
6 rooms with private bathrooms
Double: 250F
Table d'hôte: 80F per person
Open all year, Some English spoken
Region: Midi Pyrénées; Michelin Map 240

Le Balcon de Rosine is truly one of Provence's gems. When Jean Bouchet purchased the property over 30 years ago, it was a working farm. Olive trees still dot the steep incline below the shelf where the characterful 18th-century stone home stands, but the farming is now left to the Bouchets' son, for Jean is an artist. His wife, Jacqueline, offers guests a choice of two accommodations, each with its own entrance. The suite located in the main house is very nice, but my favorite is truly spectacular, occupying one end of the stone farm building where Jean has his art studio. This accommodation is like a doll's house: it has a little parlor decorated with pretty blue-and-white Provençal fabric, a small kitchen where the blue-and-white color scheme is repeated in the pottery, and a beamed-ceilinged bedroom with thick whitewashed walls, twin beds, an antique desk, and pink-and-white-striped draperies. Best of all, this suite has its own private, balcony-like terrace beneath which Provence is spread before you—a panorama of vineyards and distant hill towns, and, beyond, row upon row of mountains. If you want a romantic hideaway, this is one of the best in France—and the price is incredible for the value received. *Directions:* Take D938 from Vaison la Romaine towards Nyons for about 5 km and turn right on D46 to Puymeras, then take D205 to Mérindol les Oliviers. Go through town and take the D147 towards Propiac. Le Balcon de Rosine is on your right after 1km.

LE BALCON DE ROSINE (Gîtes de France)
Hosts: Jacqueline & Jean Bouchet
Route de Propiac
26170 Mérindol :Les Oliviers, France
Tel & fax: 04.75.28.71.18
www.karenbrown.com/france/lebalconderosine.html
2 rooms with private bathrooms
Double: 280F–340F
No table d'hôte
Closed Aug, Good English spoken
Region: Provence; Michelin Map 245

Your charming hosts at La Lumière, Beth and Peter Miller, are English. They moved to France when Peter took early retirement from IBM and purchased a piece of land surrounded by vineyards, fruit trees, and fields of fragrant lavender in one of Provence's most idyllic regions. It took several years to get permission to build, but the struggle was definitely worthwhile. Today they have a charming, blue-shuttered, Provençal-style home nestled in a wooded glen of pines and olive trees, with a beautiful small swimming pool reached by a shaded garden path. They offer one guest suite which includes a prettily decorated sitting room with floral curtains and a small well-equipped kitchen corner for making tea, coffee or a picnic. An open wooden staircase leads up from the sitting room to the sleeping loft which has a queen-sized bed. The suite has its own entrance opening onto a flagstone terrace with table and chairs shaded by an umbrella. Beth has a great flair for decorating and her home is truly a small gem. She is trained as a chef and organizes week-long wine appreciation and cooking classes. *Directions*: Take D938 from Vaison la Romaine towards Nyons for about 5 km and turn right on D46 to Puymeras, then take D205 to Mérindol les Oliviers. After La Gloriette restaurant, turn right on CR10, go 650 meters, and La Lumière is on the right in a wooded garden.

LA LUMIÈRE (Gîtes de France)
Hosts: Beth & Peter Miller
Quartier Les Grand Vignes
26170 Mérindol Les Oliviers, France
Tel: 04.75.28.78.12, Fax: 04.75.28.90.11
www.karenbrown.com/france/lalumiere.html
1 suite with private bathroom
Double: 320F
Table d'hôte: 120F per person, includes wine
Open mid-Apr to mid-Oct, Fluent English spoken
Children over 4 accepted
Region: Provence; Michelin Map 245

When the Schlumbergers bought Les Grand' Vignes over 30 years ago, it consisted of two derelict 19th-century farmhouses. François Schlumberger, a talented architect, has done a superb job of renovation, resulting in one charming stone farmhouse accented by brown shutters. Your delightful hostess, Chantal Schlumberger, is a real professional, being one of the first to open her home to guests over 16 years ago. She offers two immaculate, simply decorated guestrooms, one of which is a studio with kitchenette. In the garden there is a large swimming pool which guests may use. Also in the garden a kitchen with a refrigerator, barbecue grill, and dinnerware are thoughtfully provided—frequently guests fix themselves a light dinner here. However, the most outstanding feature of Les Grand' Vignes is its stunning setting on a hilltop, dotted with olive trees and fragrant with the scent of lavender. From the terrace where breakfast is served there is an unforgettable, panoramic view and a vineyard so close you can touch the grapes as you sip your morning coffee. *Directions*: Take D938 from Vaison la Romaine towards Nyons for about 5 km and turn right on D46 to Puymeras, then take D205 to Mérindol les Oliviers. Soon after La Gloriette restaurant, turn right on D147—Route de Mollans. The house is the first on the right.

LES GRAND' VIGNES (Gîtes de France)
Hostess: Chantal Schlumberger
Quartier Les Grand Vignes
26170 Mérindol Les Oliviers, France
Tel and fax: 04.75.28.70.22
www.karenbrown.com/france/lesgrandvignes.html
2 rooms with private bathrooms
Double: 290F–340F
No table d'hôte, Well behaved children accepted
Open all year, Good English spoken
Region: Provence; Michelin Map 245

Homelike Provençal charm abounds in the Maridors' contemporary villa located in northern Provence. Madame Maridor built her home in a typical regional style with a burnished-tile roof, warm-toned exterior walls, and an interior of cool tile floors and white plaster walls. She has decorated her guest bedrooms with curtains and bedspreads in the dainty and colorful prints typical of the Provence region and added pretty watercolors on the walls and some country antique furniture to create a fresh, feminine feeling throughout. A two-bedroom suite is offered in the main house, while an adjoining annex has two additional bedrooms, each with an independent entrance and private shower and WC. Breakfasts and table d'hôte dinners are usually enjoyed in the quiet back garden and are friendly, family meals. The swimming pool is a welcome feature on hot Provençal days. A stay with Madame Maridor means modern comfort and fastidious attention to detail, as she is a solicitous hostess who makes sure her guests' every need is fulfilled. *Directions:* From the A7 (Valence to Aix en Provence) exit at Bollène and go east following signs to Nyons. About 30 km after leaving Bollène, turn right on D4 for 6 km to Mirabel aux Baronnies. Leave the village on D160 in the direction of Villedieu as directed by Chambres d'Hôtes signs—1 km later the Maridors' driveway is on the left.

LA SARRIETTE (Gîtes de France)
Hostess: Madame Mireille Maridor
Route de Villedieu
Mirabel aux Baronnies
26110 Nyons, France
Tel and Fax: 04.75.27.14.83
www.karenbrown.com/france/lasarriette.html
2 rooms, 1 suite, with private bathrooms
Double: 320F
Table d'hôte: 90F per person, includes wine
Open Mar to Oct, Very little English spoken
Region: Provence; Michelin Map 245

The Manoir de Soubeyrac has been in the Rocca family for many generations, but it is only in recent years that Claude Rocca renovated it into a bed and breakfast. The rustic farmhouse has been tastefully restored, keeping all the lovely beams and exposed stone walls while adding deluxe bathrooms complete with Jacuzzis. The bedrooms display beautiful thick walls of stone, age-mellowed terra-cotta floors, and beamed ceilings. Antique beds with comfortable mattresses, good lighting, and nice pictures on the walls complete the ambiance of elegant simplicity. The same mood of a country home is continued in the attractive breakfast room with its large fireplace dominating exposed stone walls and small tables with French-country wooden chairs. From the moment you enter the walled inner courtyard, every detail is perfect. The bountiful display of flowers is meticulously tended, the floors freshly scrubbed, the windows sparkling. A path through an arched stone portal leads to an idyllic meadow where a large swimming pool is surrounded by white lounge chairs. Sweeping vistas extend in every direction from this haven of tranquillity in the Périgord. *Directions:* From Agen go north on N21 to Villeneuve and take D676 northeast to Monflanquin. Take D272 from Monflanquin towards Monpazier for 2 km and turn left on the C3, signposted Envals. Go approximately 3 km and turn left at the sign for Le Soubeyrac.

MANOIR DU SOUBEYRAC (Gîtes de France)
Host: Claude Rocca
Envals, 47150 Monflanquin, France
Tel: 05.53.36.51.34, Fax: 05.53.36.35.20
www.karenbrown.com/france/manoirdusoubeyrac.html
4 rooms, 1 suite, with private bathrooms
Double: 480F–550F Suite: 800F–870F
Table d'hôte: 130F per person
Open all year, Very little English spoken
Region: Périgord; Michelin Map 235

The 18th-century Manoir de Clénord is an absolute jewel—a truly superb manor in the heart of the Loire Valley, ideally situated for exploring the rich selection of châteaux in the region. The interior exudes an ambiance of lived-in comfort with handsome family heirlooms combined with flair and impeccable taste. The dining room, located in the oldest wing of the house, is stunning, with beamed ceiling and a huge fireplace. In the center of the room is a fabulous trestle table, mellowed with the patina of age, where guests sit down together family-style for delicious meals. A wooden staircase leads to the guestrooms, each individual in decor, which exude quiet elegance and refined charm. Quality wall coverings color-coordinate with fabrics used on the drapes and beds. The suites are especially elegant. If you are on a tight budget, there is one lovely little room (barely big enough for a double bed) that offers a real bargain. In addition to the manicured formal gardens and surrounding forest, guests can enjoy a large, beautiful swimming pool and tennis court. The owner, Christiane Renauld, is a warm, gracious hostess. The Manoir de Clénord is highly recommended. *Directions:* From Blois go south 10 km on D765 towards Cheverny and Romorantin. At Clénord, turn left at the sign for the Manoir de Clénord. The entrance is signposted on your left.

MANOIR DE CLÉNORD (Gîtes de France)
Hostess: Christiane Renauld
Route de Clénord
41250 Mont Près Chambord, France
Tel: 02.54.70.41.62, Fax: 02.54.70.33.99
www.karenbrown.com/france/manoirdeclenord.html
4 rooms, 2 suites, with private bathrooms
Double: 400F–700F Suite: 850F–1,200F
Table d'hôte: 160F–190F per person, includes wine
Open Apr to Nov, Very good English spoken
Credit cards: all major
Region: Loire Valley; Michelin Map 238

When Louise-Albert and Philippe-Maurice bought the Château de la Bourdaisère, their mother couldn't understand why they wanted it—the family already had three châteaux. But I can appreciate their motivation—the Château de La Bourdaisère is indeed a real beauty. A private lane leads up a small hill to the pastel-yellow stone château accented by steep gray-slate roof, gables, and turrets. A wide terrace wraps around two sides, dropping off to a lower terrace dotted by sculpted gardens. Surrounding the château are acres of forest laced with paths leading to a swimming pool and tennis court, another to the wildlife park, another to the formal rose gardens. The brothers intend to completely revamp the gardens to be a showplace for the Loire Valley. However, do not wait: the gardens as you see them today are beautiful and the interior is already restored and furnished with antiques that reflect the grandeur of days gone by. The suites are especially dramatic. The King Henry IV room is very large and has stone walls set off nicely by red carpet and silk spread and draperies. *Directions:* From Tours, take the D751 towards Amboise for 10 km to Montlouis-sur-Loire. Just after the bridge as you come into town, follow the many signs directing you to the château.

CHÂTEAU DE LA BOURDAISÈRE (Gîtes de France)
Hosts: Prince Louis-Albert de Broglie
  & Prince Philippe-Maurice de Broglie
25 Rue de la Bourdaisère
37270 Montlouis-sur-Loire, France
Tel: 02.47.45.16.31, Fax: 02.47.45.09.11
www.karenbrown.com/france/chateaudelabourdaisere.html
12 rooms with private bathrooms
Double: 660F–1,210F Suite: 910F–1,210F
No table d'hôte
Open all year, Fluent English spoken
Credit cards: MC, VS
Region: Loire Valley; Michelin Map 232

The Château de Montmaur is a designated historic monument dating from the 14th century. Found in a small village surrounded by tree-covered hills and mountains, the castle is built on a grand scale, with thick stone walls and two great halls. Authentic wood floors, fresco paintings, and huge fireplaces all testify to the castle's colorful past as a fortress, a royal castle, and even a headquarters for resistance fighters during World War II. The Laurens family are dedicated to breathing life into their historic home and have opened the large halls to public tours, weddings, classical music concerts, receptions, and parties. Parts of the castle are still being restored and five intimate suites have been completed for bed and breakfast guests. The rooms are prettily decorated with elegant fabrics and wallpapers and each has a private shower and WC as well as an independent entrance. Breakfast is served in the Laurens' charming salon/dining room which has a beamed ceiling and a lovely stone fireplace and is decorated with country antiques and fresh-flower bouquets. *Directions:* From Genoble take N75 south to Serres where you take N94 east in the direction of Gap. Go through Veynes and in about 4 km turn left following signs for Montmaur: the castle gate is clearly marked at the entry to the village.

CHÂTEAU DE MONTMAUR (Gîtes de France)
Hosts: Elyse & Raymond Laurens
Montmaur
05400 Veynes, France
Tel and fax: 04.92.58.11.42
www.karenbrown.com/france/chateaudemontmaur.html
5 suites with private bathrooms
Double: 450F
No table d'hôte
Open all year, No English spoken
Region: French Alps; Michelin Map 245

Le Relais du Lac Noir is a truly a gem. Not that the accommodations are deluxe—quite the contrary: the bedrooms are simple, and although most have a private washbasin and toilet, all share showers "down the hall." However, the rustic ambiance is charming, the mountaintop setting breathtaking, and the price incredibly low. The chalet is newly constructed, using antique timbers so that it blends with the authentically old huts on the mountain. To reach this mountain paradise, you take a very narrow road that climbs from the valley floor, up and up and up through a thick forest until the road ends at the door of Le Relais du Lac Noir. In front, tables are set for guests to take their meals when the weather is warm. On chilly days, they eat inside in a cozy, rustic-style room with beamed ceiling, warmed by an open fireplace. The same ambiance continues upstairs where the bedrooms are fresh and clean, with an appealing mountain-cabin look. The rooms usually reserved for children are really cute, with cheerfully painted bunk beds. Your charming young host is Caulliez Thierry, who when finished with his culinary training, advertised for a place to work in the mountains. He certainly found what he was looking for! He even lives right next door to the hotel in an adorable hut used by the farmers when they came up the mountain to tend their cows. *Directions:* Located about 40 km southeast of Chambéry. Follow signs to Saint Jean de Maurienne and Torino. From the N6 take the Randens exit and follow Bis D72 up the mountain for 14 km.

LE RELAIS DU LAC NOIR
Host & Chef: Caulliez Thierry
Tiouléve, 73220 Montsapey, Aiguebelle, France
Tel: 04.79.36.30.52, Fax: 04.79.36.37.80
www.karenbrown.com/france/lerelaisdulacnoir.html
8 rooms, 5 with toilet & washbasin
Double: 480F, includes breakfast & dinner
No Table'Hôte; restaurant, Credit cards: MC, VS
Closed Nov 15 to Dec 15, Good English spoken
Region: Haute-Savoie; Michelin Map 244

La Varinière is an exceptionally lovely and remarkably low-priced bed and breakfast ideally located near the Normandy beaches. This pretty bourgeois home, set in beautiful rolling green countryside, has been lovingly restored by Pippa and David Edney who used to own a successful restaurant in their native England. From the moment you arrive, you cannot help noticing that everything is impeccably kept, from the tidy gardens to the polished furniture and sparkling windows. David and Pippa completely renovated La Varinière, created the lovely garden, wallpapered all the bedrooms, put in bathrooms, sewed drapes, and slipcovered chairs. Downstairs is a riot of bold, happy colors: the entrance hall is bright blue, the parlor raspberry pink, and the dining room exuberant yellow. These colorful rooms look lovely with their coordinating fabrics. In the spacious guestrooms pretty wallpaper, attractive antique beds, and fresh flowers create a most appealing ambiance. *Directions:* From Caen take the N175 towards Mont Saint Michel and Rennes. After about 18 km turn right on the D92 towards Monts-en-Bessin. At the crossroads continue straight down the hill, take the second right, and La Varinière is the second house on the left.

LA VARINIÈRE (Gîtes de France)
Hosts: Pippa & David Edney
La Vallée
14310 Monts-en-Bessin, France
Tel: 02.31.77.44.73, Fax: 02.31.77.11.72
www.karenbrown.com/france/lavariniere.html
5 rooms with private bathrooms
Double: 280F
No table d'hôte
Closed Christmas, Fluent English spoken
Region: Normandy; Michelin Map 231

When on holiday in France, Marjorie and Brian Aylett (who are English) bought Le Presbytère on a whim. In a matter of three days they were the owners of a magnificent 15th-century rectory next to a picturesque 11th-century village church. There was no plumbing, no water, barely any electricity—only potential. Their transformation is now complete and today their lovely home is warmly furnished with comfortable antiques. There are three spacious bedrooms, each decorated in excellent taste with loving attention to detail. The bathrooms are color-coordinated, beautifully tiled, and enjoy the fluffiest of towels and several large bars of soap. The views from the property are wonderful—uninterrupted fields bordered by trees creating a patchwork of pastoral delight. Like the home, the gardens are now an oasis filled with beautiful flowers, green lawns, and patches of shade trees where benches have been strategically placed in quiet nooks. Marjorie even has her own vegetable garden where she grows produce for the evening meals. Be sure to request the table d'hôte—Marjorie is an excellent cook. Le Presbytère is truly perfection. You could pay twice the price and not experience the charm and quality of this utterly delightful bed and breakfast. *Directions:* Heading south from Paris on A6, take the Bierre les Semur/Saulieu exit onto D980 towards Saulieu, then take the D26 for 10 km to La Motte Ternant. Le Presbytère is on the high point of the village to the right of the church.

LE PRESBYTÈRE
Hosts: Marjorie & Brian Aylett
La Motte Ternant
21210 Saulieu, France
Tel: 03.80.84.34.85, Fax: 03.80.84.35.32
www.karenbrown.com/france/lepresbytere.html
3 rooms with private bathrooms
Double: 370F–390F (2-night minimum)
Table d'hôte: 130F per person, includes wine
Open all year, Fluent English spoken, no smoking
Region: Côte d'Or; Michelin Map 243

The Château de La Grand Noë is truly a gem—the idyllic setting, the superb decor, and the genuine warmth of welcome are just what you've always dreamed of finding. The castle, dating back to medieval times, has been in the same family since 1393. You enter through stately gates into a manicured front garden overlooked by the handsome two-story château with intricate brick trim decorating the windows, a steep, gray-slate roof punctuated with gabled windows, and a profusion of tall chimneys. Behind the château horses frolic in the meadow. As you walk up the steps into the reception hall, you feel you have entered into the exquisite home of a friend. Throughout there are beautiful draperies, family portraits, English-style slipcovered sofas, and heirloom antiques. A staircase leads to the guestrooms. All are lovely but my favorite of the three is a large room decorated in tones of pale peach, soft green, and yellow. Pascale de Longcamp is a woman of amazing talents: not only did she decorate the rooms, sew all the drapes, make the bedspreads, and wallpaper the rooms, but she also tiled the bathrooms herself. The most exquisite room in the house is the gorgeous 18th-century oak-paneled dining room, where Madame again stars as a superb cook. *Directions:* Take N12 from Paris towards Alençon. At Carrefour/Saint Anne go south on D918 towards Longny au Perche for 4.5 km then turn left towards Moulicent. The château is on your right in less than 1 km.

CHÂTEAU DE LA GRANDE NOË (Gîtes de France)
Hosts: Pascale & Jacques de Longcamp
61290 Moulicent, France
Tel: 02.33.73.63.30, Fax: 02.33.83.62.92
www.karenbrown.com/france/chateaudelagrandenoe.html
3 rooms with private bathrooms
Double: 500F–600F
Table d'hôte: 220F per person, includes wine
Open Easter to Nov (winter by reservation), Good English spoken
Region: Normandy; Michelin Map 231

I had seen photographs of the Château de Colliers, a handsome two-story, buff-colored château with white trim and gray mansard roof, but upon arrival I was in for a wonderful surprise—I had not realized that the château is perched on a terrace overlooking the River Loire. What bliss in the morning to open wide the casement windows, hear the birds sing, and see the river flow by below. A path just below the terrace following the river's edge is perfect for those who like to start the day with an early-morning stroll or jog. The château once belonged to the Marquis of Vaudreuil (Governor of Louisiana and French Canada until 1779). It has been in the same family since that time and thus the furnishings are authentic antiques—nothing contrived in a decorator-perfect way, just old-fashioned comfort. Family portraits adorn many of the walls—it is fun to ask just who they are. Each of the bedrooms is unique in decor, each filled with antiques. If you arrange ahead for table d'hôte, you are in for a treat—the food is excellent and served family-style in the beautiful dining room. There is a small raised swimming pool at the front of the château. *Directions:* From Blois, cross the Loire and take D951 northeast towards Orleans. Before reaching the town of Muides-sur-Loire, you see the château on your left.

CHÂTEAU DE COLLIERS (Gîtes de France)
Hosts: Marie-France & Christian de Gelis
41500 Muides-sur-Loire, France
Tel: 02.54.87.50.75, Fax: 02.54.87.03.64
www.karenbrown.com/france/chateaudecolliers.html
5 rooms with private bathrooms
Double: 550F–700F Suite: 700F–800F
Table d'hôte: 250F per person, includes wine
Open all year (winter by reservation)
Very good English spoken, Credit cards: MC, VS
Region: Loire Valley; Michelin Map 238

The Manoir de Montflambert, a 17th-century manor house hugging the edge of the forest of Reims, fronts onto a simple farmhouse courtyard. It is only after entering the home that one of its nicest aspects is revealed—behind the house is a large walled garden with a wide expanse of lawn bordered by carefully manicured beds of flowers. This grassy area stretches out to a quiet pond in a wooded glen. Inside, both the dining room and parlor take advantage of the garden view. The dining room is especially attractive, dominated by a large fireplace and handsome dark paneling which, appropriately for the Champagne region, is banded by a design of intricately carved grapes. A graceful 350-year-old staircase of polished wood winds up from the entry hall to the bedrooms, each with walls covered in a corduroy-like velour of a different hue. *Directions:* From the A4 (Paris to Reims) take the Château Thierry/Soissons exit and continue east on N3 to Épernay. From Épernay, cross the river and take D1 east towards Ay and Mareuil where you take the turnoff north to Mutigny. The Manoir de Montflambert is signposted with a Chambres d'Hôtes sign and also the name Rampacek.

MANOIR DE MONTFLAMBERT (Gîtes de France)
Hostess: Renée Rampacek
51160 Mutigny, Marne, France
Tel: 03.26.52.33.21, Fax: 03.26.59.71.08
www.karenbrown.com/france/manoirdemontflambert.html
5 rooms, 2 suites, with private bathrooms
Double: 450F–650F Suite: 600F–650F
Open Mar 15 to Nov 15, Very little English spoken
Region: Champagne; Michelin Map 237

This is a lovely, intimate château which still vibrates with the warmth of a family home. The Mascureau family grew up here and their photos tell a story of the laughter that must have echoed up the circular stone stairway. Off the entry is a handsome dining room where guest meals are served by prior arrangement. You enter into the salon on the other side where large oil paintings of previous generations look down on the sitting area. Upstairs, on the first landing are two handsome armoires and an impressive collection of pistols. The spacious bedrooms look out over the grounds and enjoy nooks and crannies tucked under the eaves and bathrooms nestled in the turrets. Two of the bedrooms have adjoining rooms without bath, convenient for a family. One is a child's fantasy—tucked in the turret round. On the grounds is a lovely family chapel. The first of many daughters was married, not in the chapel, but in the town church, and when I asked if rooms would return to the family with the promise of grandchildren, I was informed that there were many rooms to be occupied in this stately château that I did not see. Madame de Mascureau is a beautiful hostess, very gracious, very warm. *Directions:* Located 20 km northwest of Le Mans. From the A81, take the Le Mans-Ouest exit. At Coulans-sur-Gée, go in the direction of Conlie for 6 km. After the village of Saint-Julien, you will see a path on the right to the château.

CHÂTEAU DE LA RENAUDIÈRE
Hosts: Monsieur & Madame de Mascureau
72240 Neuvy en Champagne, France
Tel: 02.43.20.71.09, Fax: none
4 rooms, 3 with private bathrooms
Double: 990F
Table d'hôte: 200F per person, includes wine
Open May 15 to Oct 15, Some English spoken
Region: Northern Loire Valley; Michelin Map 232

Madame Gourlaouen's property enjoys a tranquil location near the spectacular coastline and beaches of southern Brittany and the artist community of Pont Aven. This picturesque port town is the former home of many French impressionist painters, as well as Paul Gauguin. Madame Gourlaouen is a young, capable hostess who offers bed and breakfast as well as apartment accommodation in her pretty stone farmhouse. Dating from 1730, the long, low house is built from the golden-hued stones that are typical of the Concarneau, Pont Aven region. An independent entrance leads to the guest bedrooms which are furnished with antique reproductions. Rooms are small but charming and all have private WC and shower—a great bargain for the money. The intimate breakfast room is full of charm with a low, beamed ceiling, old stone hearth, country antiques, and fresh garden flowers. *Directions:* Nevez is located approximately 30 km southeast of Quimper. Leave the town of Pont Aven on D70 towards Concarneau, turning left just outside town following signs to Nevez. In the village of Nevez, continue past the church, then take the left fork in the road onto D77 towards Port Manech. After about 4 km, just before entering Port Manech, look for a Chambres d'Hôtes sign directing you to turn right. Continue following signs, turning at the first left, and you will arrive at this sunny farmhouse 300 meters from the sea.

CHEZ GOURLAOUEN (*Gîtes de France*)
Hostess: Yveline Gourlaouen
Port Manech, 29920 Nevez, France
Tel: 02.98.06.83.82, Fax: none
www.karenbrown.com/france/chezgourlaouen.html
6 rooms with private bathrooms
Double: 240F–250F
No table d'hôte
Open all year, Some English spoken
Region: Brittany; Michelin Map 230

If not for determination, we would never have found this lovely château. Set in a meadow, accessed from the closest public road by a long gravel-and-dirt path, far from any city, and a good distance from the neighboring hamlet, Château de Dobert is truly off the beaten path. It has everything a castle should have: a moat, a bridge, turrets, and hallways filled with items that promise stories of five generations of the du Peyroux family. This is their family home and they offer three guestrooms which are located down one long hallway cluttered with paintings, old books, chairs, and tables. Each room has been decorated with family furnishings and enjoys the quiet of the rural setting. You can overlook the moat from the windows of a lovely room with a double bed decked with a blue spread. This room also has a small alcove furnished with a child's bed. A grand twin-bedded room overlooks the gardens and a first-floor apartment is spacious, with the convenience of an adjoining children's room, decorated in a charming blue-and-white motif. Breakfast is served in a formal sitting room on the first floor. *Directions:* Traveling southwest on the D309 from Le Mans, turn north on the D57 at Parcé-sur-Sarthe to Avoise. In Avoise cross the bridge to the south of town, travel up a small road, and turn right at the first street at the top of the hill. Château de Dobert is down on the left of this small country road.

CHÂTEAU DE DOBERT
Hosts: Monsieur & Madame du Peyroux
Avoise, 72430 Noyen-sur-Sarthe, France
Tel: 02.43.92.01.52, Fax: 02.43.92.16.16
www.karenbrown.com/france/chatreaudedobert.html
3 rooms with private bathrooms
Double: 610F–660F
Table d'hôte: 200F per person, includes wine
Open May to Nov, Very little English spoken
Region: Northern Loire Valley; Michelin Map 232

The Domaine Comtesse Michel de Loisy is a winner, if for no other reason than for the experience of staying with Comtesse Michel de Loisy. She is a remarkable lady of the old school—radiating refinement, yet exuding vim and vigor. At an age when many are content to sit sipping tea, she is extremely active as a certified wine-maker and as a tour guide (she owns vineyards and a winery and organizes wine-tastings and visits to cellars). Because her family has been one of the principal wine producers in the Côte d'Or for many generations, it is not surprising that she has so many fascinating stories to tell. Being a guest in her 17th- to 18th-century mansion is like staying with a friend and taking a step back in time. While her lovely home has been renovated and added onto over the years, it still retains the faded elegance of a bygone era, full of knickknacks, family portraits, and family heirlooms. One of my favorite guestrooms, the Boudoir, was formerly the Comtesse's mother's dressing room. It is very pretty with a beige-striped wallpaper, antiques, family photographs, and an en-suite bathroom. *Directions:* From Dijon take the N74 towards Beaune, exiting for Nuits-Saint Georges. Proceed into town and after the third traffic light, turn left on N74 (also named Rue Generale de Gaulle). Suggestion: When you come to the large fountain, park your car and walk the one block to 28 Rue General de Gaulle (on the right-hand side of street, behind a dark-green gate).

DOMAINE COMTESSE MICHEL DE LOISY
Hostess: Comtesse Michel de Loisy
28 Rue General de Gaulle (Route N74)
21700 Nuits-Saint Georges, France
Tel: 03.80.61.02.72, Fax: 03.80.61.36.14
www.karenbrown.com/france/domainecomtessemicheldeloisy.html
5 rooms, 4 with private bathrooms
Double: 500F–850F
No table d'hôte
Open Mar 20 to Nov 20, Fluent English spoken, Credit cards: MC, VS
Region: Burgundy; Michelin Map 243

The Chez Langlais is a hidden jewel. From the outside, the house looks nondescript and the neighborhood rather ho-hum, but once you enter through the white side gate into the back garden, the scene is magically changed. You are surrounded by a garden filled with flowers and fruit trees and the property, which looks small from the front, stretches all the way out to a tiny river. The home itself takes on a whole new dimension: seen from the back, the white house with steeply sloping roof and gables is as cozy as can be. White tables and chairs are set out under the trees, an oasis where guests gather after a day of busy sightseeing to relax and share their experiences. The living room, with its beamed ceiling and exposed stone walls, offers a cozy retreat in front of the fire for breakfast (unless the day is warm when guests usually eat outside). A narrow, handsome antique staircase leads upstairs to the bedrooms, each lovingly decorated by Martine, who sewed everything herself. The fabrics and wall covering are all color-coordinated. My favorite is the Green Room with a darling floral-print wallpaper, airy white curtains, and a view out over the back garden. However, it is not the decor or the ambiance that makes a stay here such a delight: Martine and George Langlais truly love having visitors, pampering them as if they were long-time family friends. *Directions:* Onzain is on N152 between Blois and Tours. From Onzain, take D58 west. Just after leaving town, watch for a Citroën shop on your right and, on your left, the Chambres d'Hôtes sign.

CHEZ LANGLAIS (*Gîtes de France*)
Hostess: Martine & George Langlais
46 Rue de Meuves, 41150 Onzain, France
Tel: 02.54.20.78.82 or 06.07.69.74.78, Fax: 02.54.20.78.82
www.karenbrown.com/france/chezlanglais.html
5 rooms with private bathrooms
Double: 340F–360F
Table d'hôte (occasionally): 150F–280F, includes wine
Closed Jan & Feb, Very good English spoken
Region: Loire Valley; Michelin Map 238

Plaisance (located about 30 minutes from the Paris CDG airport) is a heavenly spot to begin or end your holiday in France. Better yet, spend both your first *and* last nights here—plus a few more. Relax in total luxury and be pampered by charming Françoise Montrozier—for a fraction of the cost of a hotel in Paris. Plaisance is an adorable, ivy-covered, 13th-century stone cottage, accented by white shutters and a walled garden with lush lawn and beautifully manicured beds of flowers. In the main house there is one large bedroom elegantly decorated in a color scheme of peach and a second smaller bedroom with wood paneling. But splurge and request the deluxe room across the courtyard. This gorgeous room sets all standards for luxury and refinement. The room with satellite TV is decorated in pretty tones of pink and rose—a color scheme repeated from the beautiful fabric on the headboards to the sofa, lampshades, drapes, and carpet. The bathroom (like the one in the main house) is incredibly splendid, with fixtures of superb quality. Breakfast, a masterpiece of perfection, displays once again Françoise's (formerly of Maxim's in Paris) passion for excellence. This lodging is truly superb! *Directions:* Located about 20 km northeast of Paris CDG. From the airport take D401 to Dammartin-en-Goele, then D64 to Othis where you follow signs to Beaumarchais. Go straight and watch for the Chambres d'Hôtes sign on the right. Ask for a map.

PLAISANCE (Gîtes de France)
Hostess: Madame Françoise Montrozier
12 Rue des Suisses
BeauMarais, 77280 Othis, France
Tel: 01.60.03.33.98, Fax: 01.60.03.56.71
www.karenbrown.com/france/plaisance.html
3 rooms, 2 with private bathrooms, No smoking
Double: 450F–670F
Table d'hôte: 195F with wine, served in guests' room, No smoking
Open all year, Some English spoken by Monsieur Montrozie
Region: Île de France; Michelin Map 237

Château de Messey is one of the most perfect bed and breakfasts in our guide—absolutely outstanding in every way. To begin with, the region is gorgeous—especially fascinating for wine buffs as this is the heart of the Chardonnay wine producing district. Also, the bed and breakfast's setting is of fairy-tale quality—the adorable stone house, banked by flowers and accented with green shutters, nestles on the edge of a tiny mill stream where a weeping willow shades a rowboat beckoning guests for a lazy excursion. Breakfast and dinner are usually served outside in this hopelessly romantic setting. To add icing to the cake, the spacious guestrooms are all beautifully decorated in antiques and have excellent tiled bathrooms. Even if the above did not entice you to visit, the extraordinary hospitality of the Fachon family would alone suffice as reason to come. As an added bonus, Marie-Laurence is a superb cook. Although called "château," the bed and breakfast is located in a pretty building below the château where the workers used to live. Bernard works for the charming Dumont family who own the château (and the bed and breakfast) and can arrange a visit to their winery which produces a superb Chardonnay. *Directions:* Take A5 south from Beaune to the Tournus exit, then go west on D14 to Ozenay. Go through Ozenay and continue 2 km to Messey where the bed and breakfast is on your left.

CHÂTEAU DE MESSEY (Gîtes de France)
Hosts: Marie-Laurence & Bernard Fachon
Messey, 71700 Ozenay, France
Tel: 03.85.51.33.83 or 03.85.51.16.11, Fax: 03.85.32.57.30
www.karenbrown.com/france/chateaudemessey.html
3 rooms with private bathrooms
Double: 400F–500F
Table d'hôte: 90F per person
Closed Jan & Feb, Good English spoken
Credit cards: VS
Region: Burgundy; Michelin Map 243

The lovely Chauveau home enjoys an idyllic setting on a hillside overlooking the family vineyards and the distant River Vienne. The fine art of relaxing is easy to master in these luxurious and scenic surroundings where each day begins with fresh croissants and coffee or tea on the terrace overlooking the lush valley. Impeccable taste prevails in the furnishings and decor, creating an elegant country home ambiance. Madame Chauveau offers two bedrooms in her home as well as a two-bedroom poolside suite. The suite is very handsome, with stone walls, slate-tile floors, and pretty country antique furniture. Sunny yellow-print curtains and matching upholstery complete the pleasing ensemble. The Chauveaus' pool and sunbathing terrace are only steps away—perfect for an early-morning dip. Guest bedrooms in the main house are furnished in highly tasteful combinations of designer fabrics in floral motifs complemented by charming old paintings, antique chests, and beds. A stay at Domaine de Beauséjour is truly an experience to be savored. *Directions:* Chinon is located about 46 km southwest of Tours and Panzoult is approximately 12 km east of Chinon. From Chinon, take D21 to Cravant les Côteaux and continue towards Panzoult. The Domaine de Beauséjour is on the left after 2 km—the pretty, light-stone house is on the edge of the woods.

DOMAINE DE BEAUSÉJOUR (Gîtes de France)
Hosts: Marie-Claude & Gérard Chauveau
Panzoult
37220 L'Île Bouchard, France
Tel: 02.47.58.64.64, Fax: 02.47.95.27.13
www.karenbrown.com/france/domainedebeausejour.html
4 rooms, 2 with private bathrooms
Double: 450F–500F Suite: 600F–650F
No table d'hôte
Open all year, Good English spoken
Region: Loire Valley; Michelin Map 232

Robert Chappell and Stuart Shippey, who are English, were on holiday when they discovered Le Moulin Neuf. One look at this ever-so-romantic mill and they bought it on the spot. Of course, it didn't look anything like it does today—they have poured their love and great talent into creating a dream. Robert and Stuart live in an enchanting stone house on the property. Next door, a cozy cottage (dedicated to guests) has a charming lounge with yellow walls and yellow-and-green-floral drapes accenting comfortable sofas which are grouped around an enormous walk-in fireplace. There are six prettily decorated bedrooms, each with a tranquil view of the parklike grounds. Meticulously tended flowerbeds abound and the old mill stream loops lazily through lush grass dappled with shade from large trees. Completing this idyllic scene is a lovely pond. Dotting the lawn are lounge chairs where guests relax in utter peace, only occasionally disturbed by a duck waddling by, a visit from Fergie the rooster, or perhaps a nuzzle from Benji the adorable dog. Le Moulin Neuf is truly a very special bed and breakfast and the price is remarkably low for such fine quality and outstanding charm. *Directions:* From Limeuil, take the D31 for the Cingle de Limeuil. After passing the Cingle de Limeuil, continue down the hill then at the crossroads go straight on D2 towards Saint-Alvère. Fork left after 100 meters and continue about 2 km. The sign for Le Moulin Neuf is on the left-hand side.

LE MOULIN NEUF
Hosts: Robert Chappell & Stuart Shippey
Paunat, 24510 Sainte Alvère, France
Tel & fax: 05.53.63.30.18
www.karenbrown.com/france/lemoulinneuf.html
6 rooms with private bathrooms
Double: 364F
No table d'hôte
Open all year (winter by reservation), Fluent English spoken
Region: Dordogne; Michelin Map 233

Jasmine and Roger Albon came to Normandy on a lark, enticed by a tiny ad in a British newspaper about homes for sale. They had no intention of buying property, but one look at Le Moulin Girard (a characterful stone mill overlooking a pond and gurgling creek), and they returned to England, sold their house, and moved to France. Jasmine is keen on cooking, so they planned to open a small restaurant. However, after fixing up their new home, it seemed easier to slip into the local environment by opening a bed and breakfast. In the mill you find a homelike lounge where meals are served when it is too cool to eat outside. Also in the mill are three of the guestrooms. One is a small bedroom with an especially large en-suite bathroom while the other two petite bedrooms share facilities. The most commodious accommodations are in the adjacent miller's cottage where two bedrooms share a bathroom—perfect for friends traveling together. The low rates happily reflect the simplicity of the bedrooms. What will win your heart completely is the genuine charm of the Albons. An outstanding bonus is Jasmine's delicious home-cooked meals which are served family style—there is truly a house-party atmosphere. *Directions:* From Caen take N175 southwest for 76 km. At Villedieu les Poeles turn north on D999 towards Saint Lô. Turn right in Percy on the D98 (near the church) towards Tessy-sur-Vire. Go 2 km and turn right on D452 towards Le Chefresne. Le Moulin Girard is on your left after 250 meters.

LE MOULIN GIRARD
Hosts: Jasmine & Roger Albon
Le Chefresne, 50410 Percy, France
Tel & fax: 02.33.61.62.06
www.karenbrown.com/france/lemoulingirard.html
5 rooms, 1 with private bathroom
Double: 175F–275F
Table d'hôte: from 120F per person, includes wine
Open all year, Fluent English spoken
Region: Normandy; Michelin Map 231

Les Tilleuls resembles a typical English bed and breakfast—this is not surprising, as the owners, Cas and Don Hamilton, were born in England. They moved to the Dordogne a few years ago and bought Les Tilleuls, formerly the summer home of the bishops of Périgueux. You enter the house by a covered front porch cheerfully decorated with pots of geraniums and hanging plants. It is here that dinner is served in the summer. On cooler evenings, guests dine in the relaxed, homey atmosphere of the dining room. Cas and Don both enjoy cooking and together they prepare exceptionally delicious meals enhanced by herbs from their garden. A comfortable sitting room, which leads to a large terrace, is available to guests. A wide staircase curves to the upper levels where the bedrooms are located down slanting hallways which attest to the age of this historical house. My favorite is the bright and cheerful Sweet Pea bedroom with blue carpet, an antique white iron bed, a light-pine chest, barely-pink walls, and cheerful sweet-pea floral drapes and matching cushions on the window seat. It has its own bathroom just across the hall. Les Tilleuls is not fancy, nor is it meant to be. This is a homey, old-fashioned bed and breakfast offering the best commodity of all: outstanding warmth of welcome. *Directions:* From Périgueux take N89 east towards Brive-la-Galliard. When you come to Niversac, take D710 towards Les Eyzies. Turn left in Les Versannes, signposted Rouffignac. Plazac is 6 km beyond Rouffignac towards Montignac-Lascaux.

LES TILLEULS
Hosts: Cas & Don Hamilton
24580 Plazac, France
Tel: 05.53.50.80.65, Fax: 05.53.50.89.69
www.karenbrown.com/france/lestilleuls.html
6 rooms, 3 with private bathrooms
Double: 206F–281F
Table d'hôte: 95F per person, includes wine
Open all year, Fluent English spoken
Region: Dordogne; Michelin Map 233

A feeling of contentment and of continuity with days long past pervades the senses as you approach via the long, tree-shaded drive to the gates of the du Fayet de la Tours' family home. The imposing gray-stone castle is a former fortress dating from medieval times, and thus sits on a hillside affording an incomparable vista over the misty hills of the Auvergne countryside. Since their home is classified as a historical monument, some of the rooms have been kept in their original state and are open to the public for viewing. Antique furniture, wallpapers, and upholstery transport guests back in time. Guestrooms are accessed via the old tower's large winding stone staircase and are comfortably furnished. A tennis court and lovely gardens overlooking the panoramic view offer restful diversion. For all its history and grandeur, the Château de la Vigne is still very much a family home, presided over by the energetic, unpretentious Madame du Fayet de la Tour. Madame and her husband have six children who are all delightfully personable and attractive. A stay here is a peaceful experience, surrounded by the warm and friendly du Fayet de la Tour family. *Directions:* Ally is a very small village located about 50 km northwest of Aurillac. From Aurillac take D922 north to Mauriac. From Mauriac, take D681 southwest to the small hamlet of Ally, in the direction of Pléaux. Just before Ally, look for a sign and driveway on the left to Château de la Vigne.

CHÂTEAU DE LA VIGNE
Hosts: Monsieur & Madame Bruno du Fayet de la Tour
15700 Ally, Pléaux, France
Tel & fax: 04.71.69.00.20
2 rooms, 1 suite, with private bathrooms
Double: 720F–870F Suite: 870F–1,120F
Table d'hôte: 220F per person, includes wine
Open Easter to Nov 15, Some English spoken
Region: Auvergne; Michelin Map 239

Jane and Geoff Bramfitt owned a home in England in Stratford-upon-Avon with dreams of turning it into a small hotel. But one year, while on holiday in Brittany, they fell in love with a turn-of-the-century house overlooking the coast with an idyllic sandy cove just down the road. They bought it, moved to France, and in 1991 opened a bed and breakfast with three rooms (each with a sea view). Jane and Geoff are super hosts, pampering their guests and making them feel like friends of the family. They work as a team: Jane maintains high standards of housekeeping with beautifully laundered, crisp linens, quality towels, and spotlessly clean rooms while Geoff (whose mother was a chef) has a passion for cooking and prepares such delicious meals that many guests return in anticipation of what's for dinner. Seafood is one of Geoff's specialties and you will frequently find him out fishing for the evening meal—often with a guest in tow! Ty Pesketer is not fancy: just simple rooms, old-fashioned comfort, unpretentious friendliness, and great prices. The prize is the bedroom on the top floor—it has two cozy rooms of almost equal size (one is the bedroom, the other the bathroom), both with little balconies with a view. *Directions:* From N12 take D42 to Plestin les Grèves. Go through town to the stoplight then continue straight ahead, turning right at the harbor. Go about 2 km, watching for a sign on the left to Ty Pesketer.

TY PESKETER
Hosts: Jane & Geoff Bramfitt
Pors Mellec
22310 Plestin Les Grèves, France
Tel: 02.96.35.09.98, Fax: none
3 rooms, 1 with private bathroom
Double: 240F–280F
Table d'hôte: 75F per person
Open Apr to Nov, Fluent English spoken
Region: Brittany; Michelin Map 230

The Manoir de Kergrec'h, located on the northern coast of Brittany, is a superb 17th-century manor, impressively large, yet tremendously inviting—especially in early summer when a profusion of old-fashioned pink roses lace and soften the stern gray-stone exterior. The most outstanding attribute of the Manoir de Kergrec'h is its splendid setting in an enormous park that stretches to the sea, an absolute paradise for walking. When you enter into the large front hallway, to the right is a very formal, very fancy, somewhat intimidating living room. To the left is a handsome dining room with beautiful parquet floors in a herringbone pattern and a massive fireplace which soars almost to the ceiling. A spiral stone staircase, worn with the footsteps of time, winds up through the tower to the bedrooms which are most attractively decorated with color-coordinated fabrics and gorgeous antique furniture. All the bedrooms are appealing, but my particular favorite is located on the top floor. It is a real gem and especially cozy, with gabled windows and a delicate floral-print wallpaper in tones of rose and green. All of the bedrooms have large, modern bathrooms. *Directions:* Located on the northern coast of Brittany. Exit the N12 at Guingamp and go north to Treguier. From Treguier take D8 north for 7 km to Plougrescant. Turn right just beyond the quaint old church, continue a short distance, and you will see the stately manor on your right.

MANOIR DE KERGREC'H
Hosts: Vicomte & Vicomtesse Stephane de Roquefeuil
22820 Plougrescant, France
Tel: 02.96.92.56.06, Fax: 02.96.92.51.27
www.karenbrown.com/france/manoirdekergrech.html
6 rooms with private bathrooms
Double: 500F–600F Suite: 750F–900F
Table d'hôte: from 200F per person (occasionally served)
Open all year, Some English spoken
Region: Brittany; Michelin Map 230

Drive down a country lane past a field of sunflowers to arrive in the tiny hamlet of La Galèz, where friendly hosts Denise and Pierre Billat extend a warm welcome to their peaceful country home. The front garden is a glorious profusion of colorful flowers, blackberry brambles, and sweet-smelling herbs, all bordered by a hedge concealing a large vegetable garden. Nearby woods and countryside offer many footpaths for long walks or bike rides. Adjoining the main house is an inviting stone room once used for distilling cognac, now renovated into a cozy guest salon. There is also a dining room where Denise and Pierre share delicious and convivial home-cooked meals with their guests. Each of the guestrooms has a private bathroom: the ground-floor bedrooms are spacious, and the attic rooms have recently been enlarged. All the rooms are tastefully decorated in a simple country style with details such as lace curtains and flowering plants adding Denise's personal, feminine touch. *Directions:* Pouillac is located approximately 50 km northeast of Bordeaux. Take N10 north in the direction of Angoulême just past the town of Montlieu la Garde to Pouillac. Go through the village and turn left, following directions for the hamlet of La Galèze. After 1 km, look for a Chambres d'Hôtes sign on the right indicating a short driveway to the Billats' picturesque home.

LA THÉBAÏDE (Gîtes de France)
Hosts: Denise & Pierre Billat
La Galèze–Pouillac
17210 Montlieu la Garde, France
Tel: 05.46.04.65.17, Fax: 05.46.04.85.38
www.karenbrown.com/france/lathebaide.html
4 rooms with private bathrooms
Double: 270F
Table d'hôte: 100F per person
Open all year, Very little English spoken
Region: Atlantic Coast; Michelin Map 233

This particularly scenic section of Normandy is called Norman Switzerland due to its green, forested hills and valleys. Claude and Monique Chesnel live here in a pretty stone house, next door to which they have created an extremely pleasant room for bed and breakfast guests. Almost a suite, this spacious room can sleep up to four persons and is very comfortably furnished with a divan, double bed, antique armoire, wooden table, and chairs. Decor is very attractive, with soft carpets and harmonious colors. Located on the ground floor, the room is accessed through wide French doors which lend a light, airy feeling. The bathroom is sparklingly clean and extremely well equipped. For the traveler seeking great comfort in independent, peaceful surroundings, the Chesnels offer the perfect haven. *Directions:* Préaux Bocage is located approximately 16 km southwest of Caen via D8, turning left after 6 km onto D36 and continuing through Saint Honorine du Fay, until the turnoff for D171 to the left (look carefully: the sign faces the other direction). About 2 km later, turn right onto D139 towards Goupillières. One km down this road, look for a hard-to-find, homemade sign on a tree indicating Chambres d'Hôtes to the left (if you arrive at the church, you've gone too far). The next sign directs you to the right down a dead-end lane, at the bottom of which you will see the Chesnels' white gate.

LA CRÊTE AUX OISEAUX (*Gîtes de France*)
Hosts: Monique & Claude Chesnel
La Crete–Préaux Bocage
14210 Evrecy, France
Tel: 02.31.79.63.52, Fax: none
1 room with private bathroom
Double: 295F
No table d'hôte
Open all year, Some English spoken
Region: Normandy; Michelin Map 231

La Métairie Basse, a simple yet superb bed and breakfast, is just on the on the outskirts of Hameau de Prouilhe, a tranquil village nestled in the densely wooded hills of the beautiful Parc Naturel Régional du Haut Languedoc. Here your welcome will be as genuine as this working farm, where sheep are raised and chestnuts and walnuts harvested. One of the characterful stone farm buildings has been meticulously restored and is now totally for guests' use. It has a private terrace in front where Eliane serves an excellent breakfast. From the terrace, you enter into a small, spotlessly clean parlor with a kitchen on one side where guests are welcome to fix themselves a light meal. Down the hall are two meticulously kept, very attractive guestrooms. Each is similar, with thick stone walls, planked wooden-pegged floors, antique armoires, and handmade crocheted curtains. My favorite (because of its antique bed) has a handsome dresser, antique writing table, and an ever-so-pretty geranium floral fabric bedspread. Here you're truly off the beaten path, but the quality of accommodation is so exceptional that you will be amazed at the price. *Directions:* From Carcassonne take the D118 north to Mazamet and then the N112 east to Courniou. From Courniou, turn north on the D169 for 3 km towards Prouilhe. The Chambres d'Hôtes sign is well displayed marking the entrance to the bed and breakfast on the left before you reach the town.

LA MÉTAIRIE BASSE (*Gîtes de France*)
Hosts: Eliane & Jean-Louis Lunes
Hameau de Prouilhe
34220 Courniou, France
Tel & fax: 04.67.97.21.59
2 rooms with private bathrooms
Double: 260F
No table d'hôte
Open Apr to Oct, Some English spoken
Region: Haut Languedoc; Michelin Map 235

Monsieur and Madame Liné are an attractive, hospitable couple who take great pleasure in welcoming guests to their charming home in the countryside. The Linés enjoy inviting guests to share an aperitif in their airy glassed-in verandah looking out over the peaceful back garden and tennis court. An independent entrance leads upstairs to the pretty bedrooms furnished with highly polished antique beds, chests, and armoires and complementing designer wallpapers, upholstery, and curtains. Breakfast is a special treat as Madame Liné serves a copious meal complete with a special goat cheese from their nearby farm. The country breakfast room is indeed a pleasant place to linger, with its old tiled floor and stone fireplace, country antiques, and pewter collection. This is a bed and breakfast that tops our list including all the elements of comfort, reasonable price, charming decor, atmosphere, and an open-hearted welcome. *Directions:* Pussigny is located about 50 km south of Tours. From Tours take N10 south towards Chatellerault and turn right at the village de Port-de-Piles along the D5 in the direction of Pussigny. Just after crossing the river, turn left at the T junction in the direction of Pussigny. After entering the village limits, look for a Chambres d'Hôtes sign opposite La Mairie and the Linés' warm-stone house on the left.

LE CLOS SAINT-CLAIR (Gîtes de France)
Hosts: Monsieur & Madame Liné
6, Rue de la Mairie D18
Pussigny, 37800 Ste. Maure de Touraine, France
Tel: 02.47.65.01.27, Fax: 02.47.65.04.21
www.karenbrown.com/france/leclossaintclair.html
3 rooms with private bathrooms
Double: 260-290F
Open all year, Very little English spoken
Region: Loire Valley; Michelin Map 232

If you are looking for a wonderful castle, absolutely brimming with character, tucked far from the maddening crowds, the Château de Regagnac is your dream come true. The approach road winds through a forest and finally dead-ends at the Château de Regagnac. Go through the gates and into the courtyard which extends to a bluff and offers a sensational view out to forested hills. Château de Regagnac is furnished totally in family antiques, but although the decor is stunning, there is a homey ambiance—nothing seems stiff or formal. Some of the bedrooms are in the main part of the castle and others across the courtyard, but it does not matter which you reserve, they are all beautiful. Serge Pardoux is a great collector: don't miss seeing his astounding collection of lead soldiers. Madame Pardoux is a superb cook and, with advance reservation, will prepare a gourmet meal for you—the price is not inexpensive, but the meal will be memorable. Serge Pardoux who is the epitome of graciousness says, "Once a person walks through the gates, he becomes a friend, a guest in my home." *Directions:* Bergerac is located about 87 km east of Bordeaux via the D936. Head east from Bergerac on D660 for 27 km to Beaumont. Take D25 east to Cadouin, turn right on D2 towards Monpazier, then take the third small road on the left and follow signs to Regagnac.

CHÂTEAU DE REGAGNAC
Hosts: Monsieur & Madame Serge Pardoux
Regagnac, 24440 Beaumont, France
Tel: 05.53.63.27.02, Fax: none
www.karenbrown.com/france/chateauderegagnac.html
5 rooms with private bathrooms
Double: 600F
Table d'hôte: 400F per person, includes wine
Closed Jan & Feb, Fluent English spoken
Region: Périgord; Michelin Map 235

The beautiful 18th-century Château de Montgouverne is located just outside of Tours, yet it seems you are far from the city and deep in the countryside once you enter into the parklike grounds. The two-story, ivy-covered manor with steeply pitched slate roof looks straight out of a fairy tale—it is just as inviting and pretty as can be. Happily, the interior is no disappointment. The rooms continue the romantic mood, being totally furnished in handsome antiques and enhanced by opulent, swagged drapes of fine fabric framing the views from each window. Thanks to the clever long, narrow design of the house, all of the lounges and dining room have windows on two sides which capture idyllic views of the gardens. The bedrooms, too, are splendidly decorated. Several are in the main house, the rest in an adjacent building that was once used for the processing of the grapes. From the exterior, this "annex" looks much more rustic than the château, but this only makes it wonderfully surprising to find these rooms are just as elegant as those in the main house. As an added bonus after a day of sightseeing, there is a swimming pool for guests' use tucked in the garden. *Directions:* From Tours, take N152 east along the north bank of the Loire to the tiny village of Saint George. Turn left in Saint George at the Chambres d'Hôtes sign. Continue up the hill and turn right towards the château at the next sign.

CHÂTEAU DE MONTGOUVERNE (Gîtes de France)
Hosts: Christine & Jacques Desvignes
37210 Rochecorbon, France
Tel: 02.47.52.84.59, Fax: 02.47.52.84.61
www.karenbrown.com/france/chateaudemontgouverne.html
6 rooms with private bathrooms
Double: 590F–790F Suite: 790F–1,050F
Table d'hôte: (Tues & Sat) 225F per person, includes wine
Open Mar to Dec, Good English spoken
Credit cards: all major
Region: Loire Valley; Michelin Map 238

The comfort offered by the elegant Château de la Commanderie challenges that of the finest hotels. Comte and Comtesse de Jouffroy-Gonsans obviously take great pride and pleasure in welcoming guests to their historic home, which has been in the Comte's family since 1630. His gracious wife has redecorated the entire castle with impeccable taste, utilizing beautifully complementing color schemes in upholstery fabrics and wallpapers. Lovely collectibles, antiques, and objets d'art grace the bedrooms and public areas. Warm, personal touches such as bowls of potpourri, cologne, bath gels, and soaps add comfort and convenience to the modern bathrooms. In the evening, the Comte and Comtesse serve an aperitif in the salon before the fire, and then escort guests into an elegant dining room and host a delightful dinner party. A stay with the de Jouffroy-Gonsans is a chance to experience a taste of aristocratic country life. Hunting and riding parties are also available, season permitting. *Directions:* Farges-Allichamps is about 35 km south of Bourges. From Bourges, travel south towards Montluçon on N144. Turn off before the town of Saint Amand-Montrond at Bruère-Allichamps and follow signs to Farges-Allichamps. Château de la Commanderie is signposted. If approaching from the A71, take the Saint Amand exit—the château is 7 km from the freeway.

CHÂTEAU DE LA COMMANDERIE
Hosts: Comte & Comtesse de Jouffroy-Gonsans
Farges-Allichamps
18200 Saint Amand-Montrond, France
Tel: 02.48.61.04.19, Fax: 02.48.61.01.84
www.karenbrown.com/france/chateaudelacommanderie.html
9 rooms & suites with private bathrooms
Double: 700F–1,200F Suite: 1,200F
Table d'hôte: 350F per person, includes wine
Open all year (winter by reservation), Very little English spoken
Credit cards: AX, VS
Region: Berry; Michelin Map 238

When the Spaans decided upon early retirement, they left their native Holland and opened a bed and breakfast in a wealthy wood merchant's home just on the outskirts of Cognac. The pretty creamy-beige, white-shuttered villa (built in 1880) reflects the Victorian era in its multi-leveled roof-line, garrets, and fanciful trim. Liesbeth, an expert in creating beautiful handmade quilts, gives quilting lessons in a studio that opens onto the garden. Within, the house has a lived-in, comfortable, eclectic ambiance. For 20 years Albert was a ship's radio officer, and mementos of his travels are displayed throughout the house, along with Liesbeth's beautiful quilts. Each of the guestrooms is spotlessly clean and tidy, and pleasantly decorated with some antique furnishings. My favorite is the whimsical Pigeonnier room. Tucked under the eaves, it has a rocking horse that belonged to Liesbeth as a child, a handmade quilt in shades of yellow above the bed, and a painted armoire. Best of all, it has a romantic little wrought-iron balcony where you can sit and look out over the river to the Château Hennessy—what could be more appropriate when you're staying in Cognac country? *Directions:* From Cognac take the N141 east towards Angoulême for 3 km. At the roundabout east of Cognac take route D15 towards Saint Brice. Just before the first bridge turn right on a small lane and the villa is on your right after 1 km.

LES VOLLAUDS
Hosts: Liesbeth & Albert Spaans
16100 Saint Brice de Cognac, France
Tel: 05.45.32.15.56, Fax: 05.45.32.25.71
2 rooms with private bathrooms
Double: 350F
No table d'hôte
Open all year, Fluent English spoken
Region: Charente; Michelin Map 233

Saint Clar's market square is a pretty ensemble of stone arcaded buildings dating from the 14th century. This intimate place is a designated historic monument and is also the site of the old town hall: hence its name, Place de la Mairie. Nicole and Jean-Francois are an interesting, artistic couple who live in a partially restored section of the buildings on the square and offer charming bed and breakfast accommodations to travelers. To reach their home, you enter through an arched stone doorway into a wide hallway, formerly horse stables, and ascend a stairway to the next floor. All the guest bedrooms are separate from the Cournots' living quarters. Madame has decorated the rooms in a charming, attractive style utilizing cheerful Laura Ashley wallpapers and bright, fresh color schemes. Since our last visit, Madame Cournot says that all of the bedrooms have been renovated. Guests are welcome to relax in a lovely salon with a marble fireplace flanked by comfortable leather chairs and couch. Breakfast is served in the cozy kitchen with a blue-and-white-tiled floor and rustic antique furnishings. *Directions:* Saint Clar is located about 40 km south of Agen. Take N21 towards Auch, turning left at Lectoure onto D7 to Saint Clar. In Saint Clar, follow signs for Place de la Mairie.

CHEZ COURNOT (Gîtes de France)
Hosts: Nicole & Jean-Francois Cournot
Place de la Mairie
32380 Saint Clar, France
Tel: 05.62.66.47.31, Fax: 05.62.66.47.70
www.karenbrown.com/france/chezcournot.html
2 rooms, 1 suite, with private bathrooms
Double: 250F Suite: 290F
Table d'hôte: 90F per person
Reduced prices for 3-night reserved stays
Open all year, Some English spoken
Region: Tarn; Michelin Map 235

Martine and Jacques Lefebvre's romantic, ivy-clad home with creamy-white shutters and an enclosed front garden is reminiscent of a pretty English house. The inside is as attractive as the exterior. Martine Lefebvre, your charming hostess, used to own an antique shop and her cozy, picture-perfect parlor abounds with antiques, including a round table, a grandfather clock, superb armoire, and two handsome needlepoint chairs. Martine's excellent taste is also reflected in the guestrooms. My favorite, the Blue Room, has windows on both sides, capturing the first morning sun and the last evening light. The floor is terra cotta, the ceiling beamed, the furnishings antique, and the bed and windows draped in a blue-and-white fabric. The jovial Jacques Lefebvre teaches horse-and-carriage driving. If booked ahead, for a reasonable price he takes guests on an all-day sightseeing excursion by carriage, accompanied by a picnic packed by Martine. What a magical way for four or more people to explore the splendid countryside—I can hardly wait to try it. *Directions:* From Paris take the A11 southwest. Just beyond Le Mans Nord, take the A81 (towards Rennes). At the first exit (Joué en Charnie), go south on D4 to Sable/Sarthe, then take D309 (towards Angers) for 9 km to Saint Denis d'Aujou. As you near town, take the first road to the left, signposted Chambres d'Hôtes. The house is on the right.

LE LOGIS DU RAY (Gîtes de France)
Hosts: Martine & Jacques Lefebvre
53290 Saint Denis d'Anjou, France
Tel: 02.43.70.64.10, Fax: 02.43.70.65.53
www.karenbrown.com/france/lelogisduray.html
3 rooms with private bathrooms
Double: 330F–385F
Table d'hôte: 150F per person, includes wine
Open all year, Very good English spoken by Madame
Credit cards: MC, VS
Region: Pays de la Loire; Michelin Map 232

Having spent most of her life in the country, Madeleine Rousseau found living in an apartment in the city much too confining, so she bought Le Four à Pain, a 200-year-old farmhouse just on the outskirts of Saint Denis Le Ferment. The timbered home with steeply pitched roof was almost a ruin, but Madeleine has transformed it into an ever-so-pretty bed and breakfast. Large wooden gates open from the street onto a graveled courtyard and a meticulously cared-for garden. The back of the property gently slopes down the hillside where apple trees dot the green lawn. The spotlessly tidy lounge has a dining table for breakfast set at one end and a sitting area around the fireplace at the other. Wooden steps lead up to one of the two guestrooms, which is spacious and has a large bathroom. However, the choice accommodation is in the doll-house-like cottage in the garden where the bread used to be baked for the farm—one wall still has the original oven, the other walls are covered in a very pretty wallpaper of tiny red roses and spring flowers. The cottage also has a kitchenette and a quiet sitting area under the trees. *Directions*: From Paris take A15 north for about 35 km, then D915 (near Pontoise) north to Gisors, then D14 to Bezu Saint Eloi (5 km), where you turn right on the D17 to Saint Denis. After 1.4 km on the D17, in the village center, turn left at the Bed and Breakfast sign (at this place the road is close to the river). Go up the hill and Le Four à Pain is on your right.

LE FOUR À PAIN
Hostess: Madeleine Rousseau
8 Rue de Gruchets
27140 Saint Denis Le Ferment, France
Tel: 02.32.55.14.45, Fax: none
www.karenbrown.com/france/lefourapain.html
2 rooms with private bathrooms
Double: 235F–250F
No table d'hôte
Open all year, Some English spoken
Region: Normandy; Michelin Map 231

Your exceptionally gracious hosts, Denyse and Bernard Betts left their native Canada to move to the beautiful Haute-Savoie region of France. Upon arrival, they began looking for a spacious house with lots of character, in a beautiful setting, suitable for a deluxe bed and breakfast. Forty-nine houses later they found "it"—a 200-year-old Savoyard farmhouse perched on a hill between the Alps and the Jura mountains. Although Les Bruyères' heritage is a farm, there is nothing rustic about these accommodations. Each suite has a large bedroom opening onto a sitting room, antique furniture, fine mattresses, beautiful linens, spacious modern bathrooms, and elegant fabrics. One room is fresh and pretty with color-coordinating fabrics which are predominantly blue and white with accents of yellow. The second suite is ever-so-romantic, with dark raspberry-colored wallpaper which sets off to perfection an antique writing desk, green slip-covered chairs, and a lovely floral bedspread. As an added bonus, Denyse is an outstanding chef whose meals are both delicious and beautiful. *Directions:* Located between Annecy and Aix-Les-Bains. From the A41 take exit 15 towards Rumilly and almost immediately turn left onto RN201, signposted Saint-Félix. In front of the church in Saint-Félix, take the only road and just after the cemetery, turn left up the hill towards Mercy. At the statue, turn right, then immediately left, then left again into Les Bruyères.

LES BRUYÈRES (Gîtes de France)
Hosts: Denyse & Bernard Betts
Mercy, 74540 Saint-Félix, France
Tel: 04.50.60.96.53, Fax: 04.50.60.94.65
www.karenbrown.com/france/lesbruyeres.html
3 suites with private bathrooms
Double: 575F, 2 night minimum
Table d'hôte: 175F per person, includes wine
Open all year, Fluent English spoken, No smoking
Credit cards: MC, VS
Region: Haute-Savoie; Michelin Map 244

Set in the mystical marshlands of coastal Normandy, La Ferme de la Rivière is an imposing fortified farmhouse dating from the 16th century. The main entry leads directly into an old tower and up a well-worn spiral staircase to the dining room. The friendly Marie family serves dinners as well as breakfasts in this warm, inviting room with its atmospheric stone floors, walk-in fireplace, and country furniture. Bedrooms are found upstairs—most have enchanting views over the surrounding fields and marshes. Two of the bedrooms are quite large, share a bath and WC, and can be rented as a suite. The two smaller bedrooms have an intimate charm all their own, and each has a private shower and WC. All of the bedrooms are simply furnished, mostly in family antiques. La Ferme de la Rivière is a rare find, offering charming, comfortable accommodations, delicious country cuisine, peaceful scenery, and a warm family welcome. *Directions:* Saint Germain du Pert is located 28 km west of Bayeux via N13. Exit N13 onto D113 at La Cambe and take D113 south about 1 km to D124. Turn right onto D124. Go about 1 km to the Maries' gate, signposted on the left.

LA FERME DE LA RIVIÈRE (Gîtes de France)
Hosts: Paulette & Hervé Marie
14230 Saint Germain du Pert, France
Tel: 02.31.22.72.92, Fax: 02.31.22.01.63
www.karenbrown.com/france/lafermedelariviere.html
4 rooms, 2 with private bathrooms
Double: from 220F
Table d'hôte: 85F per person, includes cider
Open Apr to Nov, Very little English spoken
Region: Normandy; Michelin Map 231

Chalet Rémy is an adorable 18th-century stone-and-wood farmhouse perched way up in the mountains with a view over the valley to the extraordinary summit of Mont Blanc. A profusion of flowers surrounds the house and geraniums grace the balconies. Chalet Rémy is particularly famous as a restaurant and on sunny days, the terrace is brimming with families who have come to enjoy a wonderful meal there, surrounded by nature at its finest. The guestrooms all open onto a gallery which looks down upon the floor below. Be forewarned: the accommodations are small and quite basic—staying here is a bit like camping out in a mountain lodge. Each room has a sink, but all share showers and toilets "down the hall." If luxury is important to you, this would not be an appropriate choice, but for location and old-fashioned natural charm, this wonderful "restaurant with rooms" just can't be beaten. Chalet Rémy is owned by Madame Didier who is assisted in the management by her charming daughter, Frédérique, while her talented niece holds sway in the kitchen. *Directions:* Take D909 from Mègeve towards Saint Gervais. Just before coming to Saint Gervais, turn right on D43 signposted to Saint Nicholas and Le Bettex. Continue winding up the road, following signs for Le Bettex where you will see signs for Chalet Rémy.

CHALET RÉMY
Hostess: Mme Micheline Didier
Le Bettex, 74170 Saint Gervais, France
Tel: 04.50.93.11.85, Fax: 04.50.93.14.45
19 rooms, no private bathrooms
Double: 320F
Open all year
Credit cards: MC, VS
No table d'hôte; restaurant open daily
Good English spoken by Frédérique
Region: Haute-Savoie; Michelin Map 244

Le Moulin is a 19th-century watermill romantically perched on its own tiny island smack in the middle of the River Indre. Originally its English owners, Sue Hutton and Andrew Page, bought and renovated the characterful old mill as a holiday getaway, but one day they decided to just pack up and move permanently to the French countryside. Five bedrooms, each with its own private bathroom, are now available. Staying at Le Moulin is more like being invited for a house party than being a paying guest. However, if you like a prim and proper bed and breakfast, this would probably not be your cup of tea: there is an informal, somewhat bohemian atmosphere, with eclectic furnishings that combine in a comfortably style. Guests come back again and again to enjoy the hearty welcome and special fun of this delightful bed and breakfast. A tremendous bonus to the whole operation is the food: Andrew is a professional chef and his dinners are truly outstanding. I can't imagine anyone ever dining anywhere else when staying at the mill. Most of the meals during summer are served on the terrace with a view of the river. Sue, too, is extremely talented: she has used a flower theme in stenciling each guestroom's walls and painting its furniture (my favorite was Viola). *Directions:* Take N143 south from Loches. At Saint Jean, turn left into the village. You cannot miss the mill in the middle of the river.

LE MOULIN (Gîtes de France)
Hosts: Sue Hutton & Andrew Page
37600 Saint Jean-Saint Germain, Loches, France
Tel: 02.47.94.70.12, Fax: 02.47.94.77.98
www.karenbrown.com/france/lemoulin.html
5 rooms with private bathrooms
Double: 300F–350F
Table d'hôte: 110F per person, includes wine
Closed Dec, Fluent English spoken
Young children not accepted
Region: Loire Valley; Michelin Map 238

"Indeo" is a secluded jewel, truly a rare find for the traveler seeking decorator-perfect decor, stunning architectural design, award-winning gardens, a swimming pool hidden in a romantic walled garden, memorable dining, and genuine warmth of welcome. Nicole Henderson is an exceptionally talented interior designer and her English husband is an architect whose career has led them to exotic places around the world. Before retirement, their home for ten years was Korea. During that period Nicole collected superb Oriental artifacts which she has blended skillfully with colorful Provençal fabrics and antiques from her native France. The result is so stunning that "Indeo" has been featured in full-color spreads in many prominent home and architectural magazines. The bed and breakfast is located in a cluster of centuries-old stone farmhouses, romantically nestled in a wooded hamlet. Guests have their own charming stone cottage with artistically decorated bedrooms which are not large, but do not need to be. They share a spacious living room which is as comfortable as it is beautiful, along with a flower-laden terrace. *Directions:* From Ales take D981 southeast towards Uzès. After about 15 km, turn left on D7, then right on D339 towards Vacquieres. Turn right again at the first asphalt road and continue down the hill. After you pass under a stone archway, "Indeo" is the first house on your right, with yellow shutters and a discreet sign.

"INDEO"
Hostess: Nicole Henderson
Hameau de Vacquières
30580 Saint Just et Vacquières, France
Tel: 04.66.83.70.75 Fax: 04.66.83.74.15
www.karenbrown.com/france/indeo.html
5 rooms with private bathrooms
Double: 530F
Table d'hôte: 200F per person, includes wine
Open all year, Fluent English spoken, No children, No smoking
Credit cards: VS
Region: Languedoc; Michelin Map 245

The pretty old complex of La Croix de la Voulte is built of white regional stone and dates from the 15th and 17th centuries. All the guest bedrooms are found in an independent wing and are newly renovated with much attention to detail. A high level of comfort prevails; each room has a private bathroom, soft Pakistani carpets covering the stone floors, and luxurious bedding to assure a good night's sleep. Each room has a private entry and special character all its own. Anjou, the largest bedroom, is very regal, with a massive old stone fireplace, four-poster bed, old armoire, and tapestry chairs. Another is more feminine in decor, with rich rose-colored wallpaper, matching curtains, and complementing bedspreads. Low, beamed ceilings, light-stone walls, and lovely antique furniture add historical character to all the bedrooms. There is a tranquil courtyard, a park with a pond, and a sunny terrace in front of the swimming pool, a pleasant place to enjoy a leisurely breakfast. Guests may also elect to pamper themselves by bringing ice buckets and glasses that they find in their rooms to the poolside to enjoy a drink. *Directions:* Saint Lambert des Levées is located about 5 km west of Saumur on the north bank of the Loire. Take D229 in the direction of Saint Martin de la Place and Château de Boumois. Pass the Saumur train station and continue 4 km until you see the sign "La Croix de la Voulte" directing you to turn into a driveway on the right.

LA CROIX DE LA VOULTE (Gîtes de France)
Hosts: Helga & Jean Pierre Minder
Saint Lambert des Levées
49400 Saumur, France
Tel & fax: 02.41.38.46.66
4 rooms with private bathrooms
Double: 420F–520F
No table d'hôte
Open Easter to Oct, Fluent English & German spoken
Region: Loire Valley; Michelin Map 232

Le Moulin d'Inthe, hugging the banks of the River Sarthe, has an idyllic setting. While the mill dates back several hundred years, most of what you see today is an ingenious reconstruction by Claude Rollini. For three months he hauled stones from the riverbed, which he used (along with old beams, bricks, and antique paneling) to rebuild the mill. The result is a charming cottage-style bed and breakfast with gabled windows accented by a red-tiled roof. Within there is a cozy parlor with a large window looking out to the slowly turning waterwheel. Most of the bedrooms overlook the old mill pond and an enchanting view of the meandering river. Ask for the corner bedroom decorated in soft pinks and greens for it has captivating views in two directions. Jackie prepares a breakfast with homemade jams, and Claude (who was a chef in Chicago for two years) prepares dinner. Don't be surprised while dining if several ducks waddle by the dining-room window. In addition to sweet accommodations and ever-so-friendly hosts, there is another bonus—fishing along a 2.5 km stretch of the Sarthe river where trout and pike abound. *Directions:* Head southwest from Paris on A10/A11 to Le Mans, then turn north on N138 in the direction of Alençon. When you come to Beaumont-sur-Sarthe, take the D39 to Fresnay-sur-Sarthe, and the D15 to Saint Leonard des Bois. As you enter the village, take the first road on your left to Le Moulin d'Inthe.

LE MOULIN D'INTHE (Gîtes de France)
Hosts: Jackie & Claude Rollini
72590 Saint Leonard des Bois, France
Tel & fax: 02.43.33.79.22
5 rooms with private bathrooms
Double: 350F–390F
Table d'hôte: 100F per person, includes wine
Open all year, Good English spoken
Region: Normandy; Michelin Map 231

La Pastourelle is a low, stone farmhouse whose style is typical of the Brittany region. A pleasing construction is formed by gray stones of varying sizes mortared together in a seemingly haphazard manner: in fact it is easy to pick out one large boulder that was simply left in place and incorporated into the front wall of the house. The Lédés live in a separate wing of their pretty farmhouse, offering guests an independent entry, salon, dining room, and five guest bedrooms. A charming, country ambiance is felt throughout, created by Madame's collection of lovely antiques and special touches such as wildflower bouquets. The bedrooms are spotlessly clean and tastefully decorated with dainty flower-print wallpaper, softly colored carpets, and crocheted bedspreads. Delicious table d'hôte dinners are served downstairs in the cozy dining room and often include local fish or grilled meats and regional specialties such as crêpes. *Directions:* Saint Lormel is located approximately 66 km northwest of Rennes, near the town of Plancoet. From Plancoet, travel north on D768 for 1 km, then turn left onto D19 towards Saint Lormel. Before reaching the village, look for Chambres d'Hôtes signs indicating La Pastourelle which will lead to the Lédés' Breton farmhouse.

LA PASTOURELLE (*Gîtes de France*)
Hostess: Madame Lédé
Saint Lormel
22130 Plancoet, France
Tel & fax: 02.96.84.03.77
www.karenbrown.com/france/lapastourelle.html
5 rooms with private bathrooms
Double: 250F–280F
Table d'Hôte: 90F per person
Open Mar to Nov 15, Very little English spoken
Region: Brittany; Michelin Map 230

The Château de Vergières' magic begins as you approach by way of a tree-lined lane ending at the stately, three-story manor whose pastel façade is accented by white-shuttered windows and heavy-tiled roof. The rather formal exterior belies the warmth of welcome one finds within. For many years the château has been in the family of Marie-Andrée who has opened her heart and home to guests from all over the world. She is ably assisted by her gracious husband, Jean Pincedé. Inside as well as outside, the château reflects the patina of age and has an ambiance of homey comfort. Quality country antiques are everywhere, yet nothing is contrived, cutely redone, or decorator-perfect. The dining room is especially outstanding with its beamed ceiling, fabulous antique armoires, sideboard, and long wooden table surrounded by Provençal-style wooden chairs. Be sure to plan ahead so you can have the fun of sharing a meal here with your fellow guests. Since our original visit, a swimming pool has been added. Note: Château de Vergières has received an award from the World Wildlife Fund for its protection of nature (binoculars, books, and lists of birds, insects, and plants are available for the use of guests). *Directions:* Exit A54 at Saint Martin de Crau (exit 11), take D24 towards Fos sur Mer. After 3 km, watch for a sign on the right side of the road to Vergières. Turn left at the sign. Continue for 3km to the lane leading to the château.

CHÂTEAU DE VERGIÈRES
Hostess: Marie-Andrée Pincedé
Vergières, 13310 Saint Martin de Crau, France
Tel: 04.90.47.17.16, Fax: 04.90.47.38.30
E-mail: vergiere@gulliver.fr
www.karenbrown.com/france/chateaudevergieres.html
6 rooms with private bathrooms
Double: 850F–950F
Table d'hôte: 310F per person, includes wine
Open all year, Very good English spoken, Credit cards: all major
Region: Provence; Michelin Maps 240, 245

Michel and Josette Garret are former prize-winning dairy farmers who extend a warm, sincere welcome to their farm in the pastoral region north of Bordeaux. Their farmhouse is built in the typical regional style: long and low, of pretty warm-toned stone. They have completely renovated the interior, preserving the heavy-beamed ceilings, exposing the light-stone walls, and adding cool tiled floors and modern conveniences. Sharing an avid interest in local history and regional antiques, they have filled their home with lovely old pieces such as a huge Bordeaux armoire, a Louis XIV mantelpiece, and a cherry-wood grandfather clock. Bedrooms are prettily furnished and enhanced by French doors leading out to bucolic pasture lands. An additional bedroom with private bathroom has been added in a converted outbuilding. *Directions*: Saint Martin de Laye is located 45 km east of Bordeaux. Leave Bordeaux on the N89 towards Libourne. Then take D910 to Saint Denis de Pile where you turn left at the *mairie* (town hall) onto D22 going over the bridge towards Bonzac. After Bonzac continue on D22 for 1.8 km then turn to the right on a small road marked Gaudart Buisson. Go 700 meters to a Chambres d'Hôtes sign and turn left—the Garrets' house is 200 meters farther on at the end of the driveway.

CHEZ GARRET (Gîtes de France)
Hosts: Josette & Michel Garret
Saint Martin de Laye
33910 Saint Denis de Pile, France
Tel: 05.57.49.41.37, Fax: none
www.karenbrown.com/france/chezgarret.html
3 rooms with private bathrooms
Double: 180F–250F
Table d'hôte: 85F per person, includes wine
Open end of Apr to Oct, No English spoken
Region: Atlantic Coast; Michelin Map 233

Claudine is the busy mother of two children, but runs her bed and breakfast with quiet efficiency and professionalism. The two-story white stone house, located just across the street from the Loire, has belonged to late husband's family for over 150 years. Behind the house there is a garden where Claudine grows fresh vegetables for her home-cooked dinners, and beyond it stretch acres of apple and pear orchards. Inside, the house is basic: a central hallway that opens to a dining room on the left which also has a lounge area with sofa and chairs for guests. There are four bedrooms upstairs in the main house, each with its own bathroom. Ask for the corner bedroom in the back. It has a pretty floral-print wallpaper, an antique bed, a beautiful armoire, and windows on two sides which make it especially bright and cheerful. Two more double rooms and a suite were added in 1996 in a separate building facing the back courtyard. For those of you who do not expect everything to be decorator-perfect and like the idea of sharing the family home of an exceptionally gracious, hard-working young hostess, Le Bouquetterie makes a very good choice. *Directions:* From Saumur, take D952 west along the Loire for 25 km. About 1 km after the center of Saint Mathurin-sur-Loire, you see the Claudine Piniers' home on your right.

LE BOUQUETTERIE (Gîtes de France)
Hostess: Claudine Pinier
118, Rue du Roi Rene
49250 Saint Mathurin-sur-Loire, France
Tel: 02.41.57.02.00, Fax: 02.41.57.31.90
www.karenbrown.com/france/lebouquetterie.html
7 rooms with private bathrooms
Double: 290F–340F Suite: 530F
Table d'hôte: 120F per person, includes wine
Open all year, Good English spoken
Region: Loire Valley; Michelin Map 232

The 16th-century prince of poets, Ronsard, wrote some of his greatest love sonnets to Marie at the Manoir du Port-Guyet. However, the characterful stone house had fallen into sad disrepair when it was purchased by Madame Valluet Deholin. The house, built in the 15th century as a hunting lodge for the Abbaye de Bourgueil, was never meant to be a fancy home and the charming Madame Valluet Dehoin, who welcomes guests into her home as friends, has taken great care to maintain the original ambiance. The patina of fine-quality antique furniture contrasts beautifully with the original walls and floors. Massive fireplaces attest to days long ago when hunters gathered before the open fire to warm themselves after a day's sport. Although the walls are very thick, the home is sunny and cheerful as light streams in through tall casement windows. There are three bedrooms authentically furnished in antiques. *Directions:* From Samur head east on N152 for abut 20 km and turn north to Bourgueil. From Bourgueil take D35 west to Saint Nicolas. About 700 meters beyond the church, turn left at a small street signposted Port Guyet. Almost immediately there is a road to the left. Do NOT take this, but continue down the hill for about 300 meters to where the road splits. Turn left here and you will see the gates to the Manoir du Port-Guyet immediately on your right with a brown-and-white sign saying "Historical Monument."

MANOIR DU PORT-GUYET (Gîtes de France)
Hostess: Geneviève Valluet Deholin
37140 Saint Nicolas de Bourgueil, France
Tel: 02.47.97.82.20, Fax: 02.47.97.98.98
3 rooms with private bathrooms
Double: 550F–750F
Table d'hôte: 220F per person, includes wine
Open Apr to Nov, Very good English spoken
Region: Loire Valley; Michelin Map 232

Monsieur and Madame Lawrence are an interesting, well-traveled couple who enjoy a healthy, outdoor lifestyle in the Provençal region. Their lovely, golden-toned stone house is set on a tranquil hillside overlooking a breathtaking vista of vineyards and green hills. Guests have a separate entrance through French doors off a shady terrace. The guest bedroom has a mezzanine area for a third person, and is very tastefully decorated with a mixture of contemporary and antique furniture, Oriental rugs, and a subtle color scheme. Some unusual and fascinating pieces (such as a carved wooden chest from the Lawrences' travels in Bali) provide attractive accents to the room's decor. A spotless and well-equipped bathroom completes the comfortable accommodation. *Directions:* Saint Pantaléon is located approximately 40 km east of Avignon. Take N100 in the direction of Apt, turning left at the village of Coustellet. At Coustellet take the direction of Gordes. After Les Imberts, take a right in the direction of Saint-Pantaléon towards Gordes. After passing the hamlet of Les Imberts, turn right (D207 and D148), following signs towards Saint Pantaléon. Pass the church, staying on D104 for 50 meters farther, turn up the first small up hill road on the left, and the second driveway on the right leads to the Lawrence home.

VILLA LA LEBRE (*Gîtes de France*)
Hosts: Monsieur & Madame Lawrence
Près de Saint Pantaléon
84220 Gordes, France
Tel & fax: 04.90.72.20.74
www.karenbrown.com/france/villalalebre.html
1 room with private bathroom
Double: 260F
No table d'hôte
Open all year, Good English spoken
Region: Provence; Michelin Maps 245, 246

La Ferme des Poiriers Roses is an absolute dream. This quaint Normandy farmhouse features a picture-perfect façade—crooked wood beams, cream-colored plaster, steep roof enhanced by gabled windows, and blue windowboxes spilling over with pink geraniums. The home is even more incredible inside—a virtual fantasy of flowers. Every nook and cranny is highlighted by huge, exquisitely arranged bouquets of fragrant fresh flowers. In addition, an unbelievable assortment of dried flowers, cleverly tied with pretty ribbons, hang from the rough-hewn beamed ceilings, creating a whimsical canopy of color. All the flowers come from the garden and are dried and arranged by Elizabeth and her three daughters. Each of the cozy bedrooms has its own personality and shows Elizabeth's loving hand and artistic flair. There are antique accents in each of the bedrooms and, of course, flowers, flowers, flowers. Best of all are the owners whose happy nature permeates their little inn—the entire family opens their hearts to you in an unsurpassed welcome. I should not close without mentioning the breakfast—no, I will leave that as a surprise. *Directions:* From the A13 (Rouen to Caen) take the Lisieux exit. From Lisieux go north on D579 for about 5 km to Ouilly-le-Vicomte where you turn right on D98 signposted to Saint Philbert. Go about 4 km, turn right on D284. The farm is on the first road on your left.

LA FERME DES POIRIERS ROSES
Hosts: Elizabeth & Jacques Lecorneur
14130 Saint Philbert des Champs, France
Tel: 02.31.64.72.14, Fax: 02.31.64.19.55
www.karenbrown.com/france/lafermedespoiriersroses.html
7 rooms with private bathrooms
Double: 450F–600F
No table d'hôte
Open all year, Some English spoken
Region: Normandy; Michelin Map 231

Old mills are almost always extremely appealing, and the pretty 17th-century Le Petit Moulin du Rouvre is no exception. The picturesque stone building with steeply pitched, dark slate roof nestles in a lush grassy garden next to a small mill pond that is back dropped by a dense green forest. You enter directly into the dining room which is as cozy as can be with a cradle in front of a large fireplace. Stone walls, tiled floors, country-French table and chairs in the middle of the room, a wonderful antique armoire, and colorful plates on the walls make the room very warm and appealing. An adjacent parlor, with beamed ceiling and open fireplace is somewhat more formal in decor and has windows opening onto the pond. There are four bedrooms which are quite small and basic in decor, but immaculately clean. The choice bedroom is Les Amis, decorated in blues and with an opening where you can look below and see the old water wheel. *Directions:* From Rennes take N 137 for 40 km north towards Saint Malo. Take the Saint Pierre de Plesguen exit, then take the D10 towards Lanhelin. Before you reach Lanhelin, you see the road leading to Le Petit Moulin du Rouvre well signposted on the right side of the road. (Along the way you will see another bed and breakfast sign with another name.)

LE PETIT MOULIN DU ROUVRE (Gîtes de France)
Hostess: Annie Michel
35720 Saint Pierre de Plesguen, France
Tel: 02.99.73.85.84, Fax: 02.99.73.71.06
www.karenbrown.com/france/lepetitmoulindurouvre.html
4 rooms with private bathrooms
Double: 340F–360F
No table d'hôte
Closed Nov, Very little English spoken
Region: Brittany; Michelin Map 230

The Château de Roussillon is an old fortified castle, partially in ruins, perched on a rock outcrop high above a deep valley. The existing castle and towers date from the 13th and 15th centuries, but were built on the remains of a far more ancient fortress. Madame Hourriez offers extremely romantic accommodation in the ancient tower chapel. The large guestroom has a private bath and an independent entrance off the upper stone courtyard. A high stone-vaulted ceiling and exposed stone walls lend a very medieval feeling to this spacious room furnished entirely in dark-wood antiques, Oriental rugs, and tapestry wall hangings. A comfortable double bed is found near a window, set deep into the thick rock wall, offering a spectacular view over the valley below. A cozy fireplace corner beckons in the evenings or on cool autumn afternoons. Madame brings breakfast every morning to the room or to the outdoor table and chairs in the courtyard garden. For longer stays, Madame Hourriez has an equally picturesque, fully equipped apartment for up to six people. *Directions:* Saint Pierre Lafeuille is located about 8 km north of Cahors. Take N20 towards Paris and, once in the village of Saint Pierre, look for a sign pointing to the right for Château de Roussillon.

CHÂTEAU DE ROUSSILLON (*Gîtes de France*)
Hostess: Marcelle Hourriez
Saint Pierre Lafeuille
46090 Cahors, France
Tel: 05.65.36.87.05, Fax: 05.65.36.82.34
www.karenbrown.com/france/chateauderoussillon.html
1 room with private bathroom
Double: 400F
No table d'hôte
Open Apr to Nov 10, Very little English spoken
Region: Lot; Michelin Map 235

Hilary and Tony Prime decided to make a change from their hectic professional lives in London where Tony was a newspaper photographer and Hilary was a television announcer. While visiting friends in Aubeterre, they saw and fell in love with La Sauzade, a handsome 18th-century stone manor set in 6 acres of gardens. The house is bright and cheerful with tall windows letting in the sun. There is a light airy dining room where both Hilary and Tony are on hand with plenty of information about what to see and do in the surrounding area. A fabulous old wooden spiral staircase winds up to three guest rooms which are homey and comfortable. In the front of the manor is a large swimming pool, a welcome respite on a hot day after sightseeing. Even if you speak French, it might be a relief to slip back into English again for a few days and not have to tax your vocabulary skills. *Directions:* Saint Romain is located 95 km northeast of Bordeaux. Take the D2 east from Chalais. Just before Aubeterre, when the road forks, turn left on D10 (signposted Montmoreau). La Sauzade is about 1 km along on the left side of the road.

LA SAUZADE
Hosts: Hilary & Tony Prime
16210 Saint Romain, France
Tel: 05.45.98.63.93, Fax: none
www.karenbrown.com/france/lasauzade.html
3 rooms with private bathrooms
Double: 450F–500F
Table d'hôte: 90F per person, includes wine
Open Easter to Nov, Fluent English spoken
Region: Atlantic Coast; Michelin Map 233

The absolute magic of Maison Garance is even more dramatic because nothing from the exterior hints at the wonder you find within. All you see is a nondescript brown gate at the end of a rather scruffy alley. However, when the gate swings open, you enter into a beautiful "secret" garden, totally framed by the house and high walls. Another stunning garden stretches behind the house, highlighted by a picture-perfect swimming pool which looks out to a sweeping panorama of the Lubéron. Ask to see the "before and after" pictures of the property when the Bennetts first purchased it. You will not believe that such an ugly duckling could be transformed into a ravishing swan or that anyone would have the bravery to tackle such an awesome task of renovation. Today, everything is restored to absolute perfection and every room decorator-perfect to the smallest detail. Each of the guestrooms is charming. The more expensive ones are especially spacious and worth the extra cost. As for the food—it is exceptional—Madame Bennett is not only a talented decorator, but also a professionally trained chef. *Directions:* From Gordes take D2 east towards Saint Saturnin lès Apt. After La Tuilière, go 1.5 km, then turn left towards Bassacs. Go just up the hill—about 200 meters. Look carefully for a short alley on your right, ending in a brown fence with the sign "Garance."

MAISON GARANCE
Host: Pascal Bennett
Hameau des Bassacs
84490 Saint Saturnin Lès Apt, France
Tel: 04.90.05.74.61, Fax: 04.90.05.75.68
www.karenbrown.com/france/maisongarance.html
5 rooms with private bathrooms
Double: 550F–700F
Table d'hôte: dinner 150F, lunch 100F per person
Closed Nov 15 to Dec 27, Good English spoken
Credit cards: all major
Region: Provence; Michelin Map 245

The Auberge du Moulin de Labique sits on the rise of a hill overlooking a little creek that flows into a picture-perfect pond with lazily swimming ducks. Hélène and François Boulet-Passebon, the gracious, hard-working owners, operate the property as a farm, bed and breakfast, and restaurant where Hélène is the chef. The oldest part of their beige-stone home dates back to the 15th century. The building is typical of the area except for an amazing, two-story, columned verandah which stretches across the front, giving the effect of an ante-bellum mansion. No one can remember who added such a fanciful embellishment, but it is very old. One of the guestrooms is in the main house while the remainder are found in the old stone hay barn above the restaurant. The bedrooms are attractively decorated with pretty wallpapers, excellent country antiques, and color-coordinating fabrics—the front-facing bedroom is particularly enticing, with cheerful flower-sprigged wallpaper. In the meadow behind the house is a swimming pool. Horses frolic in a nearby field—they are beauties as François specializes in breeding fine horses (riding can be arranged). *Directions:* From Périgueux go south on N21 to Bergerac. From Bergerac take the N21 south to Castillonnès, the D2 east to Villeréral, then south towards Monflanquin for 2 km. Turn right on the D153 for 2 km to Born and south towards Saint Vivien for 2 km. Auberge du Moulin de Labique is on your left, before Saint Vivien.

AUBERGE DU MOULIN DE LABIQUE (Gîtes de France)
Hosts: Hélène & François Boulet-Passebon
Saint Vivien / Saint Eutrope de Born
47210 Villeréral, France
Tel: 05.53.01.63.90, Fax: 05.53.01.73.17
3 rooms with private bathrooms
Double: 460F
Table d'hôte Nov to May, Restaurant open May to Nov
Open all year, reservations required, Good English spoken
Credit cards: VS
Region: Aquitaine; Michelin Map 235

The flower-filled medieval village of Salers is perched on a high point in the mountainous region of central France. Officially classified as one of the prettiest villages in France, it is a picturesque jumble of quaint, cottage-style houses and shops, all built from regional gray stone and with slate roofs. Hosts Claudine and Philippe Prudent offer travelers comfortable and practical accommodation in a separate wing of their historic house. Bedrooms are all similar in decor, featuring country-style beds, tables, and chairs and small alcoves with shower, washbasin, and WC. Exposed ceiling beams and dormer windows add character to the functional rooms. Guest quarters are accessed through a peaceful green garden which has a magnificent view over the surrounding hills and valleys. Breakfast is served here in this tranquil, natural setting or, if preferred, in guest bedrooms. *Directions:* Salers is located approximately 35 km north of Aurillac. Take the N122 north from Figeac to Aurillac, then D922 north towards Mauriac on a winding, hilly road, turning right onto D680 towards Salers. Travel through the village on narrow cobblestone streets all the way to the central square. Turn left down the Rue des Nobles and look for a Chambres d'Hôtes sign marking the Prudents' house.

CHEZ PRUDENT (Gîtes de France)
Hosts: Claudine & Philippe Prudent
Rue des Nobles
15410 Salers, France
Tel: 04.71.40.75.36, Fax: none
www.karenbrown.com/france/chezprudent.html
6 rooms with private bathrooms
Double: 232F
No table d'hôte
Open all year, Some English spoken
Region: Auvergne; Michelin Map 239

Near the Spanish border, the rolling green foothills of the Pyrenees are filled with picture-book villages, including Sare. Here you find an outstanding bed and breakfast, the Olhabidea. Use this perfect hideaway as your base to explore this enticing area and also to sample a little night life in the resorts of Biarritz and Saint Jean de Luz. This lovingly restored farmhouse captures the tradition and rustic flavor of the Basque region. You cannot help being captivated by the delightful ambiance of this charming home—an old wooden settle beside the fireplace whose overmantle is trimmed with fabric, a rustic polished table laid with blue-and-white dishes, bouquets of fresh flowers, and comfortable sofas. The snug farmhouse atmosphere is further enhanced by the Basque blue-and-white color scheme and the polished flagstone floor set beneath the low, beamed ceiling. Every spacious bedroom has its own bathroom. A delicious breakfast is the only meal served by the effervescent Anne Marie. For dinner, guests often sample traditional Basque fare at the Hotel Arraya in Sare, owned by Anne Marie's sister-in-law. The hotel is a handy place for asking directions if you have difficulty finding Olhabidea. *Directions:* Exit the N2 autoroute at junction 3 signposted Saint Jean de Luz (Nord). Take the D918 through Ascain to Saint Pée sous Nivelle and the D3 towards Sare. After several kilometers (2 km before Sare) turn left when you see a small old church on the right. The bed and breakfast is signposted from here.

OLHABIDEA (Gîtes de France)
Hosts: Anne Marie & Jean Fagoaga
64310 Sare, France
Tel: 05.59.54.21.85, Fax: 05.59.47.50.41
3 rooms with private bathrooms
www.karenbrown.com/france/olhabidea.html
Double: 300F–350F
No table d'hôte
Open Mar to Nov, No English spoken
Region: Pyrénées-Atlantiques; Michelin Map 234

The Château de Sassangy, a stately 18th-century building, is a luxurious home and working farm. When André Marceau and his wife, Ghyslaine (who was born in Martinique), bought the property, both the home and the vineyards were almost derelict. Today, not only has the house been completely renovated, but quality white and red wines are once again produced from the château's vineyards. In addition to 15 acres planted in grapes, the château is surrounded by 250 acres of gorgeous rolling hills where cattle graze in tranquil, tree-traced meadows. All of the guestroom windows open to idyllic countryside vistas. Ghyslaine decorated all the rooms in different colors with matching wallpaper, draperies, and bedspreads. One of my favorites, La Bodienne, is decorated in shades of blue accented by a floral print of blues, yellows, and rust. The Marceaus are especially gracious hosts who make guests feel as if they are friends of the family. As André said, "We receive visitors as we live—well and simply." *Directions:* Take the Chalon South exit from the A6 (Paris to Lyon) towards Monceau les Mines (N80) for 16 km. Turn left towards Sassangy and after 4 km you see the château signposted on your left.

CHÂTEAU DE SASSANGY (Gîtes de France)
Hosts: Ghyslaine & André Marceau
Sassangy, 71390 Buxy, France
Tel: 03.85.96.12.40, Fax: 03.85.96.11.44
www.karenbrown.com/france/chateaudesassangy.html
6 rooms, 1 suite, with private bathrooms
Double: 550F–750F Suite: 700F–900F
No table d'hôte
Open mid-Mar to mid-Nov, Good English spoken
Credit cards: MC, VS
Region: Burgundy; Michelin Map 243

Le Prieuré Sainte Anne is a favorite on our list of bed and breakfasts, offering a warm welcome in a tranquil, appealing setting. This 15th-century cottage recalls the days of Joan of Arc with its low, beamed ceilings and exposed stone walls. Madame Caré is a motherly hostess who obviously takes great pleasure in welcoming guests to her charming, ivy-covered home. Her well-tended garden provides fresh-flower bouquets lavishly displayed throughout her rooms which are furnished in highly polished family antiques. The bedrooms in the suite are comfortable and extremely romantic, with walk-in fireplaces and charming stone window seats. Small-paned, leaded-glass windows look out over the peaceful courtyard and secret garden. A hidden path leads up to this green haven where you are tempted to spend a lazy afternoon with book in hand or simply listening to the occasional bird. It is the fortunate traveler indeed who has the chance to stay at this enchanting bed and breakfast. *Directions:* Savonnières is located about 11 km southwest of Tours on the south bank of the Loire via D7 in the direction of Villandry. Once in Savonnières, look for Chambres d'Hôtes signs that lead to Madame Caré's driveway.

LE PRIEURÉ SAINTE-ANNE (*Gîtes de France*)
Hostess: Lucette Caré
10, Rue Chaude
Joué Les Tours
37510 Savonnières, France
Tel: 02.47.50.03.26, Fax: none
www.karenbrown.com/france/leprieuresainteanne.html
1 suite with private bathroom
Double: 320F (2-night minimum)
No table d'hôte
Open all year, No English spoken
Region: Loire Valley; Michelin Map 232

Saint Jean is a most attractive, two-story buff-colored home with red-tiled roof and blue shutters, a style typical of this beautiful region of Provence. This appealing bed and breakfast, perfect for several days' exploration of Provence, has an ideal setting on a small rise of hill, a site continuously occupied since the 10th century when a monastery was built here. With her children growing older, the extremely gracious Gisele Augier decided to convert some of the space in her large home into a bed and breakfast. She now has an attractively decorated lounge exclusively for the use of guests with game tables, television, and comfortable chairs, plus three bedrooms, each with a private entrance. The immaculately kept bedrooms are very tastefully decorated with pretty color-coordinated fabrics and a few pieces of antique furniture. My favorite (the yellow bedroom) costs slightly more, but has its own little terrace with pretty white wicker chairs overlooking the garden. Behind the house is a peaceful little park with lily ponds and reflecting pools enhancing the lush lawn. Tall trees through which you can see vineyards edge the property. There is also a large swimming pool (a welcome retreat after sightseeing on a warm day) set on a terrace overlooking a field of grapes. *Directions:* From the A7 (Lyon to Aix en Provence) exit at Orange. Continue on N977 towards Vaison la Romaine. At the Seguret crossroads turn right on D88 towards Seguret. Go 800 meters then turn left: Saint Jean is the second house on the left.

SAINT JEAN (Gîtes de France)
Hostess: Gisele Augier
84110 Seguret, France
Tel: 04.90.46.91.76, Fax: none
www.karenbrown.com/france/saintjean.html
3 rooms with private bathrooms
Double: 480F–570F
No table d'hôte
Open all year, Very little English spoken
Region: Provence; Michelin Map 245

Luckily, a reader who lives in Paris shared her discovery of Le Clos des Tourelles with us and now we can pass on to you this superb find. Le Clos des Tourelles is nestled in a 17-hectare park, right in the center of Sennecey-Le-Grand. The heritage of the estate dates back to the 12th century. Today there are three buildings on the property, one being a beautiful small château with a gray-slate mansard roof. This is where you find the guestrooms—and what beauties they are, all totally furnished with fine antiques enhanced by lovely fabrics. The owner, Madame Derudder, personally decorated each one with great skill and loving care—every tiny detail is perfect. Another building is a charming timbered house, accented by two jaunty towers and a galleried walkway overhanging the terrace below. Inside is a cozy kitchen where dinner is served when there are only a few guests dining. If there are more than eight persons choosing table d'hôte, you are in for a real treat! In that case, dinner is served in a stunning medieval tower at a long table magnificently set with fine linens and crystal in front of an enormous stone fireplace. As an added bonus, there is a swimming pool in the garden. *Directions:* Take the A6 south from Beaune in the direction of Lyon. Take the Chalon-sur-Saone exit and go south on N6 to Sennecey-Le-Grand. In the middle of the village, turn to your right, following the signs to Le Clos des Tourelles.

LE CLOS DES TOURELLES (Gîtes de France)
Hostess: Madame Laurence Derudder
71240 Sennecey-Le-Grand, France
Tel: 03.85.44.83.95, Fax: 03.85.44.90.18
www.karenbrown.com/france/leclosdestourelles.html
8 rooms with private bathrooms
Double: 380F–820F
Table d'hôte: 180F per person
Open all year, A little English spoken
Region: Burgundy; Michelin Map 243

The Lethuilliers built their Norman dream house near the picturesque port town of Fécamp and the spectacular cliffs of Étretat. The entire house is furnished in lovely antiques, complemented by pretty flowered wallpapers, Oriental rugs, and fresh-flower arrangements. Madame Lethuillier proudly displays her collections of brass and copper artifacts on the living-room mantel, as well as a fine collection of old plates that once belonged to her grandmother. Madame Lethuillier is a talented seamstress and her artistic flair is evident in every room, creating a pleasing feeling of homelike elegance. Breakfast can be enjoyed either in the inviting salon (complete with tabby cat curled up on a chair cushion) or, weather permitting, on the terrace overlooking the front garden and goldfish pond. The Lethuilliers do not speak English, but their British daughter-in-law lives nearby and is happy to stop by to help with any communication difficulties. *Directions:* Senneville is located approximately 45 km northeast of Le Havre via D940 which changes to D925 after Fécamp: on D925 the route is well marked by signs for Chambres d'Hôtes. Follow a country lane bordered by wildflowers, turning right at a small sign for Val de la Mer.

CHEZ LETHUILLIER (Gîtes de France)
Hostess: Mireille Lethuillier
Val de la Mer
76400 Senneville sur Fécamp, France
Tel: 02.35.28.41.93, Fax: none
3 rooms, 2 with private bathrooms
Double: 300F
No table d'hôte
Open all year
No English spoken
Region: Normandy; Michelin Map 231

Located in the heart of the Burgundy wine region, Maryse and Philippe Viardot's charming home is an ideal base from which to explore the surrounding countryside and sample the renowned local wines. Although their 200-year-old house is found in a small village, it remains a quiet haven, set back from the street and bordered by a peaceful garden. Madame is an energetic hostess with a real flair for decoration who has managed to capture just the right blend of contemporary design and old-fashioned ambiance in her home and guestrooms. Bedrooms are highly tasteful combinations of soft color schemes, pretty country antiques, and carefully chosen artwork. Fresh flowers and plants personalize the attractive rooms, making guests feel right at home. Warm, sunny mornings mean breakfast in the garden, while in cooler weather it is served in the shelter of a pleasant, glass-enclosed verandah. *Directions:* Senozan is approximately 15 km north of Mâcon. Take the Mâcon exit from the A6 (Paris to Lyon) and go north on N6 towards Tournus, turning off after 10 km following signs for Senozan. Just after entering the village, look for a small stone church on the right. Across the street you will see a stone entryway, set back between two houses, and marked with a Chambres d'Hôtes sign. Turn left and drive through this portal to the end of the driveway, passing the houses closest to the road.

CHEZ VIARDOT (Gîtes de France)
Hosts: Maryse & Philippe Viardot
Rue du Château
71260 Le Bourg Senozan, France
Tel & fax: 03.85.36.00.96
3 rooms with private bathrooms
Double: 260F
No table d'hôte
Open all year, Very little English spoken
Region: Burgundy; Michelin Map 243

The Jezequel family offers old-fashioned hospitality and delicious farm-fresh meals at the quaint Ferme Auberge de Sepvret. Their 300-year-old home is covered with ivy and surrounded by a pretty, flower-filled garden. Farm-style meals are served in the intimate and homelike dining room furnished with round wooden tables adorned with bouquets of fresh flowers and a cheerful selection of tablecloths. Traditional home-cooked fare features regional specialties such as *farci poitevin*, a type of soufflé made from garden greens (spinach, cabbage, parsley, and sorrel), eggs, sour cream, and spices. Simple country charm is felt throughout the house and in the guest bedrooms which are furnished with brass beds, old armoires, and flowered wallpapers. Large windows open out to the back garden, letting in plenty of light and fresh air. Days usually begin with a romantic and peaceful breakfast enjoyed outdoors at a table set under the trees. *Directions:* Sepvret is located about 45 km southwest of Poitiers. Take N10 towards Angoulême for 2 km, then turn off onto N11 (which later becomes D150) and travel in the direction of Niort, La Rochelle, and Saintes. Turn right after about 40 km onto D108 to Sepvret. Once in the village, follow signs for Chambres d'Hôtes and Ferme Auberge which lead to the Jezequels' home.

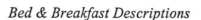

FERME AUBERGE DE SEPVRET (Gîtes de France)
Hosts: Françoise & Claude Jezequel
Sepvret
79120 Lezay, France
Tel: 05.49.07.33.73, Fax: none
www.karenbrown.com/france/fermeaubergedesepvret.html
3 rooms with private bathrooms
Double: 200F
Table d'hôte: 70F per person
Open all year, Very little English spoken
Region: Atlantic Coast; Michelin Map 233

Emile and Gilberte Moynier are wonderfully warm and solicitous hosts. Their 17th-century manor house is set back from the main road behind trees framing a magical view of the green valley and distant mountain peaks. Gilberte has decorated each of the guest bedrooms differently, combining classic country charm with her own personal artistic style. Les Hirondelles (The Nightingales) has dainty, mauve-flowered curtains and matching bedspreads on lovely old wooden beds complemented by a matching armoire, while Les Tilleuls (The Lime Trees) is bright and fresh, with hand-painted furniture and tall windows looking out over the front garden. A separate dining room/kitchen/lounge area is available for guests' use. Formerly a sheep stall, it now has a cozy ambiance created by low, vaulted ceilings and walls of exposed stone sheltering rustic country antiques and a cheerful fire blazing in the hearth. In the garden is an enticing swimming pool. *Directions:* Take the N75 south from Grenoble towards Nice. About 6 km before the village of Serres, look for signs for L'Alpillonne and a sign advertising Chambres d'Hôtes–English spoken. The Moyniers' driveway is on the left and is easy to miss.

L'ALPILLONNE (Gîtes de France)
Hosts: Gilberte & Emile Moynier
La Plaine de Sigottier
Serres, 05700 Sigottier, France
Tel: 04.92.67.08.98, Fax: none
4 rooms, 3 with private bathrooms
Double: 260F–330F
No table d'hôte
Open Jun 15 to Sep 15, Good English spoken
Region: Maritime Alps; Michelin Map 245

Le Petit Manoir, a typical two-story, stone, Normandy-style home with red-tiled roof, is flanked on two sides by farm buildings and fronted by a stone wall. From the moment you drive into the courtyard, you notice that everything is as neat as a new pin. The characterful, centuries-old stone house is brightened with climbing roses, flowerboxes at the windows, pots of geraniums, and a circular flower bed. Inside, Annick's good housekeeping is again evident, for everything is spotlessly clean and tidy. Annick's bed and breakfast occupies one wing of the house. On the ground floor is a small breakfast room—although guests usually eat outside when the weather is warm. An exterior staircase leads to two small, meticulously kept bedrooms which, although simple in decor, are very nice, with contemporary furnishings, sweet floral-pattern wallpaper, and private bathrooms. The bedrooms are almost identical, but the one facing the back has a special surprise—from the window you see cornfields stretching off to the distant shoreline and the horizon where Mont Saint Michel is clearly seen. For a budget place to stay, Le Petit Manoir offers a warm welcome and far more class and comfort than usually found at this price. *Directions:* From Caen head southwest on N175. Go through Avranches and continue on the N175 for about 12 km. Turn right at Servon and go straight into the village. When the street ends, turn right: Le Petit Manoir is down the road on the left.

LE PETIT MANOIR
Hosts: Annick & Jean Gédouin
50170 Servon, France
Tel: 02.33.60.03.44, Fax: 02.33.60.17.79
2 rooms with private bathrooms
Double: 200F
No table d'hôte
Open all year, Very little English spoken
Region: Normandy; Michelin Map 231

Le Chaufourg is truly a dream—absolute perfection. Georges Dambier has created an exquisite work of art from what was originally a rustic 18th-century farmhouse that has been in his family "forever." The task of renovation was formidable, but all the ingredients were there: the house, built of beautiful soft-yellow stone, already had charm and its location on a bend of the Isle river is idyllic. Although strategically located in the heart of the Dordogne and conveniently near access roads to all the major sights of interest, once within the gates leading to the romantic front courtyard, one feels insulated from the real world. The exterior of the house is like a fairy-tale cottage with its white shuttered doors and windows laced with ivy and surrounded by masses of colorful flower gardens. Inside, the magic continues. Each guestroom is entirely different, yet each has the same mood of quiet, country elegance, with natural stucco walls of warm honey-beige, stunning antiques, and tones of soft whites and creams. You find nothing stiff or intimidating—just the elegant harmony of country comfort created by an artist. Georges Dambier adds the final ingredient—the warmth of genuine hospitality. Another plus—superb meals are served in Le Chaufourg's exquisite restaurant. *Directions:* From Périgueux take N89 southwest in the direction of Bordeaux for about 32 km to Sourzac (about 3 km before Mussidan). You see the entrance to Le Chaufourg on the right side of the road.

LE CHAUFOURG EN PÉRIGORD
Host: Georges Dambier
24400 Sourzac, France
Tel: 05.53.81.01.56, Fax: 05.53.82.94.87
www.karenbrown.com/france/lechaufourgenperigord.html
9 rooms with private bathrooms
Double: 910F–1,360F Suite: from 1,660F
No table d'hôte; restaurant
Open all year, 2-night minimum (winter by reservation)
Very good English spoken, Credit cards: all major
Region: Dordogne; Michelin Map 233

It is a pleasure to recommend a small, homey, inexpensive bed and breakfast in a quiet location away from the mobs of tourists who congregate along the the bustling, expensive Côte d'Azur. High in the forested hills above the coast, the Meiers' contemporary home is built in the traditional Mediterranean style with a pink stucco façade, brown shutters, and a heavy red-tiled roof. Set on a heavily wooded hillside, the home offers an exceptionally tranquil atmosphere. From the living room, doors open onto a terrace neatly planted with flowers and graced by an inviting swimming pool. It is here that breakfast is served when the weather is warm. There is not a hint of commercialism to Ani's and Jean's bed and breakfast—they enjoy having company and welcome house guests into their home as "friends of the family." Their geniality is reinforced by their tail-wagging German Shepherd. One bedroom has an en-suite bathroom. The other is my favorite (even though the bathroom is down the hall) because it has such a beautiful view to the forested hills. *Directions:* Tourrettes-sur-Loup is in the hills, north of the A8, about midway between Cannes and Nice. From Tourrettes-sur-Loup, take D2210 towards Grasse for about 5 km, then take a tiny road to the left, marked Rte des Vallettes du Sud. The houses are numbered—you will find 533 on your left.

CHEZ MEIER-GAILLARD
Hosts: Ani & Jean Meier-Gaillard
533, Route des Vallettes du Sud
06140 Tourrettes-sur-Loup, France
Tel & fax: 04.93.59.25 31
www.karenbrown.com/france/chezmeiergaillard.html
2 rooms, 1 with private bathroom
Double: 270F–300F
No table d'hôte
Open all year, Little English spoken
Region: Côte d'Azur; Michelin Map 245

Domaine du Prieuré sits like a queen on her throne, nestled in the wooded hills high above the Riviera. The charming 18th-century farmhouse had fallen prey to neglect when the Millars bought it in the mid-1960s and brought it back to life. The paint was stripped to display a wonderful stone patina which looks especially pretty with the white shutters and heavy-tiled roof. In front of the house there is a stunningly romantic terrace featuring a large swimming pool. Guests are welcome to use the pool in the morning and before supper but they are expected to vacate their rooms during the day. Staying with the Millars is as close as you can get to feeling like a guest in a private home. There is a natural, unpretentious, "lived-in" ambiance with the family's personal belongings, paintings, photographs, and knickknacks about. The two guestrooms are decorated with period furniture and each has a private bathroom across the hall. The delightfully British Joanna is not only an extraordinary hostess, but a keen gardener who has made her property such a showplace that garden clubs come to visit. *Directions:* From Vence, take D2210 west to Tourrettes-sur-Loup. Go through the village and continue for 5 km. Just after a very sharp curve, take the small road on the right, signposted "Route de Courmettes." The Domaine du Prieuré is the first house on your right.

DOMAINE DU PRIEURÉ
Hostess: Joanna Millar
106 Route de Courmettes
06140 Tourrettes-sur-Loup, France
Tel: 04.93.24.18.77, Fax: 04.93.59.36.39
www.karenbrown.com/france/domaineduprieure.html
2 rooms with private bathrooms
Double: 500F–550F
No table d'hôte
Closed Jan & Feb, Fluent English spoken, No children
Region: Côte d'Azur; Michelin Map 245

The Le Rouzics' attractive, contemporary house is situated on the picturesque Trinité inlet overlooking sailboats moored peacefully between gray rock cliffs and dark-green pines. Monsieur and Madame converted part of their home into comfortable bed and breakfast accommodation with scenic views over the water and surrounding countryside. The bedrooms are sparklingly clean and furnished in a tasteful, modern style with fresh pine-wood or wallpapered walls. The Le Rouzics invite guests to make themselves at home and enjoy the television and stereo in the casual salon. An adjoining glassed-in verandah with a glorious southern exposure is a relaxing spot to enjoy breakfast above the pretty inlet. Early risers are even treated to the sight of playful wild rabbits who inhabit the surrounding fields and hedgerows. *Directions:* La Trinité sur Mer is located between Quimper and Vannes off the N165. Take N165 to Auray, then D28 towards Locmariaquer and La Trinité sur Mer. After crossing the Pont (bridge) de Kerisper, take the first right and continue straight ahead, following signs for La Maison du Latz. Take the dirt road that circles the château to the left, following it around to the right, and look for arrows directing you to Chambres d'Hôtes. The Le Rouzics' driveway and white Breton-style house will be on the right.

LA MAISON DU LATZ
Hostess: Nicole Le Rouzic
Le Latz, 56470 La Trinité sur Mer, France
Tel: 02.97.55.80.91, Fax: 02.97.30.14.10
4 rooms with private bathrooms
Double: 290F–350F Suite: 400F
Table d'hôte: 110F per person
Open all year, Very little English spoken
Region: Brittany; Michelin Map 230

Overlooking the scenic River Loire and the pastoral valley beyond, on the site where Richard the Lionheart installed his troops at the end of the 12th century, stands the stately Château de la Voûte. Termed a bed and breakfast by the owners, the quality of its comfort and the elegance of its furnishings rival some of France's loveliest châteaux. It was a treat to explore each of the five bedrooms, all with private bath, as they are individual and outstanding in their decor, having received the artful attention of both Claude and Jacques. Gorgeous antiques, handsome fabrics, lovely carpets, and original art are beautifully coordinated. Although there are no public rooms available to guests, the bedrooms have comfortable seating areas and excellent lighting. A breakfast feast is served on the garden terrace or in the bedrooms before large windows whose shutters open up to the fresh morning air. In the evening it is an enjoyable walk down the garden path and a short stroll along the village street to an outstanding country restaurant, Le Cheval Blanc. Charming, convenient, and reasonably priced, Le Cheval Blanc is a welcome bonus as the Château de la Voûte does not serve meals other than breakfast. (Chef Michel Coyault, tel: 02.54.72.58.22, closed Monday nights.) *Directions:* From Tours, take the N10 north to Vendôme and then travel west on the D917 to the village of Troo.

CHÂTEAU DE LA VOÛTE
Hosts: Claude Venon & Jacques Clays
41800 Troo, France
Tel & fax: 02.54.72.52.52
www.karenbrown.com/france/chateaudelavoute.html
5 rooms with private bathrooms
Double: 480F–580F
No table d'hôte
Open all year, Some English spoken
Region: Loire Valley; Michelin Map 238

In the heart of the château country lies the well-priced Manoir de Chaix, where you can enjoy both real country ambiance and excellent accommodations. The handsome two-story farmhouse, dating back to the 16th century, is owned by the hospitable Suzanne Fillon. She speaks no English, but you can communicate with her son and daughter, both of whom live on the farm and speak English. On the property are a swimming pool and clay tennis court (open from May to October)—if you wish, Madame Fillon's son can give you tennis lessons. Dinner is served family-style in the large dining room. A private entrance leads to the spiral stone staircase which takes you up the tower to the outstandingly decorated bedrooms—all have some antiques and headboards prettily upholstered in fabric that matches the drapes. My least favorite room is the most expensive one, so do not splurge, just take one of the standard rooms. Best of all I liked La Varidaine, a lovely gabled room overlooking the countryside room with a stunning antique armoire, and beamed ceiling. For those on a tight budget, La Touraine is a tiny but very pretty room that rents for 280F. In the morning Madame Fillon serves a delicious breakfast with fresh juice, homemade jam, and honey from the estate. *Directions:* From Tours, take N143 south to Truyes. Turn east on D45 (towards Bléré) for 3.6 km then turn right at the Chambres d'Hôtes sign.

LE MANOIR DE CHAIX (Gîtes de France)
Hostess: Suzanne Fillon
37320 Truyes, France
Tel: 02.47.43.42.73, Fax: 02.47.43.05.87
www.karenbrown.com/france/lemanoirdechaix.html
4 rooms, 1 suite, with private bathrooms
Double: 280F–330F Suite: 330F
Table d'hôte: 85F per person, includes wine
Open all year, Some English spoken
Credit cards: all major
Region: Loire Valley; Michelin Maps 232, 238

The ancient Roman town of Vaison la Romaine is found in a hilly, wooded setting in northern Provence. Just outside of town on a high point affording panoramic views of the surrounding mountains and plains, the Delesses' 150-year-old stone house offers a refined haven for travelers. The bedroom, well soundproofed by thick old stone walls, is accessible from an independent entrance. French doors lead to an intimate terrace overlooking a restful view of fields and distant hills. The room is tastefully decorated and very comfortable, with a writing table and bookcase stocked for guests' enjoyment. Monsieur and Madame are both teachers, specializing in French and English respectively, so communication is no problem and convivial breakfasts are enjoyed together in their cozy beamed breakfast room or outside in the tranquil front courtyard. A pool has been added since our visit. *Directions:* Vaison la Romaine is about 18 km north of Carpentras via D938. If coming from Avignon, follow signs to Orange, and then for Vaison la Romaine. Upon entering the town, go towards the Super V supermarket. At the traffic circle, follow sign to Nyons. At the second traffic circle, take the left and follow the road between the school and the stadium, then turn right, then left again into Chemin de l'Ioou. The Delesses' driveway is on the right and is marked with a Chambres d'Hôtes sign.

CHEZ DELESSE (Gîtes de France)
Hosts: Françoise & Claude Delesse
Chemin de l'Ioou
Le Brusquet, 84110 Vaison La Romaine, France
Tel: 04.90.36.38.38, Fax: none
www.karenbrown.com/france/chezdelesse.html
1 room with private bathroom
Double: 300F
No table d'hôte
Open all year, Very good English spoken
Region: Provence; Michelin Maps 245, 246

Vaison la Romaine, an unspoiled fortified village rising steeply from the banks of the L'Ouveze river, has a superb bed and breakfast owned by the Verdier family. Jean, an architect, and Aude, his pretty wife, moved from Paris to this ancient walled city in 1975 and worked together to transform the ruins of what was once a part of the bishop's palace into a gracious home for themselves and their three sons. There are four guest bedrooms with their own charmingly decorated lounge and a private entrance to the street. Of the guestrooms, my favorites are the twin-bedded rooms which have more of an antique ambiance than the double-bedded room with its bit of an art-deco feel. Aude serves breakfast on an enticing terrace snuggled amongst the rooftops or, when the weather is chilly, in the family dining room. Although Aude and Jean speak only a smattering of high-school English, their absolutely genuine warmth will guarantee a very special stay in this highly recommended bed and breakfast. *Directions:* Vaison la Romaine is located 45 km northeast of Avignon. When you reach the town of Vaison la Romaine, cross the river and climb the narrow road to the Ville Médiévale. L'Évêché is on the right side of the main street, Rue de l'Évêché.

L'ÉVÊCHÉ (Gîtes de France)
Hosts: Aude & Jean Loup Verdier
Rue de l'Évêché
Ville Médiévale
84110 Vaison la Romaine, France
Tel: 04.90.36.13.46, Fax: 04.90.36.32.43
www.karenbrown.com/france/leveche.html
4 rooms with private bathrooms
Double: 380F–420F
No table d'hôte
Open all year, Very little English spoken
Region: Provence; Michelin Maps 245, 246

The *Lady A* is certainly not your typical bed and breakfast—it is a barge. But the quality is so high, the warmth of welcome so genuine, and the price so low that it is a pleasure to recommend it. Lisa (who's Dutch) has been in the hospitality business for a very long time. For 20 years she chartered sailboats in the Mediterranean and the Caribbean before moving to France where she and her husband refitted the *Lady A* to charter on the Burgundy canals. Nowadays the 100-foot barge moves no more but remains moored on a charming small canal in an absolutely beautiful setting—beneath Châteauneuf, an extremely picturesque walled village crowning the nearby hill. The colorful barge is lots of fun. You quickly become friends with the other guests in a house-party atmosphere. Each of the three staterooms has a private bathroom (the shower is not enclosed, but is adequate). The bedrooms (as would be expected on a boat) are just big enough for two beds (which can be made into a king-sized bed), a closet, and shelves for clothes. When not sleeping or exploring Burgundy, guests spend most of their time on the deck—a great place to enjoy a drink in the twilight and watch the action of the other boats on the waterway. *Directions:* From the A6 take the Pouilly-en-Auxois exit through Créancy to Vandenesse (D18)— *Lady A* is moored in the basin to the left of the road.

LADY A (*Gîtes de France*)
Hostess: Lisa Jansen Bourne
Port du Canal, Cidex 45
21320 Vandenesse-en-Auxois, France
Tel: 03.80.49.26.96, Fax: 03.80.49.27.00
www.karenbrown.com/france/ladya.html
3 rooms with private bathrooms
Double: 280F
Table d'hôte: 90F per person
Open Feb to Dec, Fluent English spoken
Region: Côte d'Or; Michelin Map 243

Villa Velleron had been abandoned for 40 years when Simone and Wim bravely bought the property. During restoration, they discovered treasures such as a beautiful stone wall no one knew existed and clues to the building's varied heritage—they found an old olive press and racks used for the processing of silk. Simone Sanders is a well-known Dutch industrial designer, so it is not surprising that there is such exceptionally artistic perfection in every detail of the house, dramatically blending old and new. There is a stunning swimming pool romantically nestled on a terrace bordered by picturesque stone walls, and an inner courtyard that simply oozes charm—potted geraniums, ivy-draped walls, fragrant roses, and lush lawn make every niche a dream. It is in this enclosed garden that guests enjoy both breakfast and dinner at small tables draped in pretty Provençal-print fabric. Although the sitting and dining rooms have a decidedly Provençal charm, each of the bedrooms follows a specific theme which varies all the way from art-deco to Oriental. Simone's husband, Wim, who is in charge of the kitchen, is also exceptionally talented. Several major magazines have featured the outstanding food, imaginative decor, and the architectural design of the Villa Velleron. *Directons:* From Carpentras take D49 south to Velleron. Villa Velleron is in the center of Velleron, down a small lane, catty-corner across the square from the post office.

VILLA VELLERON (Gîtes de France)
Hosts: Simone Sanders & Wim Visser
Rue Roquette
84740 Velleron, France
Tel: 04.90.20.12.31, Fax: 04.90.20.10.34
www.karenbrown.com/france/villavelleron.html
6 rooms with private bathrooms
Double: 500F–590F
Table d'hôte: 150F per person
Open Easter to Nov, Fluent English spoken, Children over 8
Region: Provence; Michelin Map 245

In French, La Maison aux Volets Bleus means The House of the Blue Shutters—indeed, the bright cobalt shutters of the Marets' charming home can be seen from far below the hilltop town of Venasque. Follow a winding road up from the plains to this ancient town which is now a haven for painters and art lovers. An old stone archway leads to the Marets' romantic walled garden and their picturesque home filled with colorful dried-flower bouquets hanging from every available rafter. The cozy living room opens onto a balcony with a sensational panoramic view. Each bedroom is unique and decorated with Martine Maret's artistic flair for harmonious colors, Provençal prints, and simple, attractive furnishings. Martine and her husband Jerome are an energetic couple with many talents who enjoy welcoming guests into their home and to their table. Plan to stay for several days to enjoy genuine hospitality and delicious meals. *Directions:* From the A7 take the Avignon North exit following signs northeast to Carpentras. From Carpentras take the D4 towards Apt for 8 km and turn to Venasque. Look for the turnoff marked Venasque to the right up a hill. Continue to the fountain square (Place de la Fontaine) and look for a Chambres d'Hôtes sign down the road a little to the left indicating the arched entry to the Marets' home.

LA MAISON AUX VOLETS BLEUS (Gîtes de France)
Hosts: Martine & Jerome Maret
Place des Bouviers
Le Village, 84210 Venasque, France
Tel: 04.90.66.03.04, Fax: 04.90.66.16.14
www.karenbrown.com/france/lamaisonauxvoletsbleus.html
6 rooms with private bathrooms
Double: 350F–420F Suite: 680F
Table d'hôte: 120F per person
Open Mar 15 to Nov 1, Good English spoken
Region: Provence; Michelin Maps 245, 246

Domaine de Montpierreux is one of the budget entries in our guide. However, do not judge this bed and breakfast by its room rates, for this 19th-century farmhouse has great charm. A small lane leads up through the fields to the large, two-story house whose buff-colored façade is accented by white shutters. The farm is owned by the gracious Françoise and François Choné who warmly welcome guests into their home. Handsome family antiques accent the simple, yet most attractive rooms on the ground floor. At the end of the hall, a staircase spirals up through the tower to five bedrooms tucked under the steeply pitched roof. Each of the bedrooms has a cozy quality created by open beams and gabled windows. The impeccably kept rooms are simple in decor, yet attractive, with individual color schemes. On the same floor as the guestrooms, there is a lounge and game room which can be combined with a bedroom to make a family suite. Behind the house, a shaded path leads through the forest to a vineyard from which the Chonés harvest grapes and produce wine. There are also truffle grounds on the property. If you'd like to experience a working farm, you will find Domaine de Montpierreux a real winner. *Directions:* From the A6 exit at Auxerre Sud and follow the D965 in the direction of Chablis for 3 km. The lane leading to the Domaine de Montpierreux is signposted off the D965 to your right.

DOMAINE DE MONTPIERREUX (Gîtes de France)
Hosts: Françoise & François Choné
Domaine de Montpierreux
Route de Chablis, 89290 Venoy, France
Tel: 03.86.40.20.91, Fax: 03.86.40.28.00
www.karenbrown.com/france/domainedemontpierreux.html
5 rooms with private bathrooms
Double: 270F–300F Suite: 330F
No table d'hôte
Open all year, Very little English spoken
Region: Burgundy; Michelin Map 237

The attractive and friendly Porret family offer travelers comfortable accommodations in a newly renovated part of their chalet-style house. Monique and Joseph paid close attention to detail when remodeling their guest quarters, adding welcome conveniences such as a pine-paneled kitchen and completely independent entry. The four guest bedrooms are all very similar, each with a private bathroom and French doors leading to a private balcony. A fresh, clean feeling pervades the rooms which are tastefully decorated with warm textured wall coverings and contemporary furniture. La Cascade is an ideal stopping place for travelers seeking reasonably priced accommodations with modern comfort in the heart of the scenic French Alps. *Directions:* From Lyon take A43 east to Chambéry and then A41 north to Annecy. Vesonne is approximately 30 km south of Annecy via N508 in the direction of Albertville. About 3 km before the town of Faverges, look for a sign for Col de la Forclaz (Forclaz Pass) to the left that leads through the village of Vesonne. Go through the village, following signs for Col de la Forclaz. Just after crossing a bridge, look for the Porrets' driveway on the left marked with a Chambres d'Hôtes sign.

LA CASCADE (Gîtes de France)
Hosts: Monique & Joseph Porret
83 Chemin de la Forge
Vesonne
74210 Faverges, France
Tel: 04.50.44.65.48, Fax: none
www.karenbrown.com/france/lacascade.html
4 rooms with private bathrooms
Double: 210F–270F
No table d'hôte
Open all year, No English spoken
Region: French Alps; Michelin Map 244

The fairy-tale-like Château du Riau, although charmingly small, happily lacks none of the accoutrements of a proper castle. A bridge spans the ancient moat and leads through a whimsical, twin-towered keep (fashioned from bricks arranged in a fanciful diamond design) into the enclosed courtyard. Facing the courtyard, the two-story manor house with steep gray-slate roof reflects a harmonious blend of styles from the 15th, 16th, and 17th centuries. The present Baron and Baronne Durye are descendants of the original owner, Charles Papillon, a goldsmith from Moulins, who received the property from Anne de Beaujeu, daughter of King Louis XI. Although a historical monument and at times open to the public for tours, the castle is definitely a family home, occupied by the Duryes and their three sons. Reached by an impressive circular stone staircase, the bedrooms are beautifully appointed in fine antiques and all look onto a tranquil forest. My favorite, a large corner room with pretty blue-and-white wallpaper, is especially bright and cheerful. Throughout the house, family portraits and memorabilia abound. I particularly enjoyed the portrait of one portly ancestor who, it turns out, was an officer who fought in the American Revolution with Lafayette. *Directions:* From Moulins take the N7 north towards Nevers for 15 km. Just after the dual carriageway changes to two lanes, you see the lane to the château signposted to your right.

CHÂTEAU DU RIAU (Gîtes de France)
Hosts: Baron & Baronne Joseph Durye
03460 Villeneuve-sur-Allier, France
Tel: 04.70.43.34.47, Fax: 04.70.43.30.74
www.karenbrown.com/france/chateauduriau.html
3 rooms with private bathrooms
Double: 650F
Table d'hôte: 200F per person, includes wine
Open all year, Good English spoken
Region: Centre Bourbonnais; Michelin Map 238

When Christine and Xavier Ferry bought Ferme du Château, 25 kilometers west of Reims, it looked absolutely hopeless: no water, no electricity, cows and pigs living in the house. However, with the help of family and friends, they transformed the derelict house back into a proper home. Christine and Xavier have boundless energy. He runs the farm and, when cows became unprofitable, he turned the grazing ground into an 18-hole golf course. (Energetic guests will also enjoy the tennis court on the grounds.) Christine is a busy mother, yet manages to offer four of her nicely decorated bedrooms to the public. She is also an exceptionally good chef and prepares an evening meal except on weekends, a time she sets aside to be with her children. From the front, the building looks like a farmhouse flanked by stone barns but from the rear garden with its own little stream, the house looks quite different: more like a small, turreted castle. *Directions:* From the A4 (Paris to Reims) take the Dormans exit. Turn right towards Dormans, right again back over the expressway towards Villers Agron, then right at the first road which leads to the Ferme du Château.

FERME DU CHÂTEAU (Gîtes de France)
Hosts: Christine & Xavier Ferry
02130 Villers-Agron, France
Tel: 03.23.71.60.67, Fax: 03.23.69.36.54
www.karenbrown.com/france/fermeduchateau.html
4 rooms with private bathrooms
Double: 350F–420F
Table d'hôte: 165F per person, includes wine
Open all year, Fluent English spoken
Region: Champagne; Michelin Map 237

The 13th-century Château de Villiers-le-Mahieu fulfills any childhood fantasy to live in a fairy-tale castle. The beautifully maintained castle sits in parklike grounds, manicured to perfection, on its own little island surrounded by a moat. The main access is over a narrow bridge leading into the inner courtyard-garden, framed on three sides by the ivy-covered stone walls of the château. The Château de Villiers-le-Mahieu is not a homey little castle where one becomes chummy with the owners, but rather a commercial operation with 18 guestrooms in the château and 11 in the garden annex. Splurge and request room 1, a grand room in the original castle, wallpapered in a handsome blue print fabric which repeats in the drapes at the three tall French windows looking out to the gardens. In the park surrounding the castle there is a superb swimming pool and tennis courts. *Directions:* Located 40 km southwest of Paris. Take the A13 west from Paris and exit south on A12 toward Dreux-Bois d/Arcy. Continue following the signs to Dreux until you come to Pontchartrain, then take D11 signposted to Thoiry. As the road leaves Thoiry, turn left on D 45 toward Villiers le Mahieu and continue through the town—you will see signs to the château on the left side of the road.

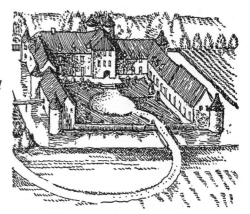

CHÂTEAU DE VILLIERS-LE-MAHIEU
Host: Jean-Luc Chaufour
78770 Villiers-Le-Mahieu, France
Tel: 01.34.87.44.25, Fax: 01.34.87.44.40
www.karenbrown.com/france/chateaudevillierslemahieu.html
29 rooms with private bathrooms
Double: 705–870F
Table d'hôte: on request–6 person minimum*
*From 320F per person
Credit cards: AX, VS
Open all year, Good English spoken
Region: Ile-de-France; Michelin Map 237

Monsieur and Madame Portal's contemporary home is found on a scenic plateau high above Aix les Bains, with spectacular views over the surrounding granite peaks. In this tranquil setting guests are two steps away from lovely walks on the wooded plateau, yet at the same time have the convenience of close-by civilization. Madame Portal is a very warm, cheerful hostess who makes sure her guests feel comfortable and at home. Bedrooms, attractively furnished in a contemporary style, all open onto a balcony above the Portals' restful garden and many have a nice view of the lake. The house is built on a hillside and there is a lower level where the Portals have installed a fully equipped kitchen so that guests may prepare their own evening meals. A flagstone terrace with a table and chairs opens out to the garden for a pleasant dinner setting. *Directions:* From Lyon take A43 to Chambéry. You can go to Viviers du Lac by either N491 or N201. When you arrive in the village where there is a fountain, town hall, and church, take the Route des Essarts. Go straight for 700 meters, follow the curving road up a hill, weaving right when the road forks. At the top of the hill, look for the Portals' brown gate on the left (1193 Route des Essarts).

CHEZ PORTAL (Gîtes de France)
Hosts: Monsieur & Madame Portal
1193 Route des Essarts
73420 Le Viviers du Lac, France
Tel: 04.79.61.44.61, Fax: none
3 rooms, 1 with private bathroom
Double: 300F
No table d'hôte
Open all year, Some English spoken
Region: French Alps; Michelin Map 244

James and Marie-Jose Hamel are an exceptionally friendly couple who take great pleasure in welcoming guests to their manor home. Originally a fortress dating from the 12th century, Le Château was rebuilt in 1450 and again in 1750 and has a colorful history. The Hamels are fond of recounting the story of their most famous visitor, Andy Rooney of *Sixty Minutes* fame. Rooney worked here as a journalist during World War II when the château was inhabited by the American Press Corps and revisited in 1984. Breakfast is served in the former press room complete with brass nameplate in English still intact on the door. A lofty ceiling, dark, pine-paneled walls, and a lovely old tile floor provide intimate surroundings to begin the day or enjoy an evening aperitif. Guest bedrooms are tastefully furnished and decorated with handsome antiques and harmonious color schemes. The rooms are found in a separate wing of the château, thus affording guests a convenient, private entry. *Directions:* Vouilly is located approximately 25 km west of Bayeux. Take D5 west to Le Molay Littry, then turn right, continuing on D5 in the direction of Isigny-sur-Mer until you reach Vouilly. Just after entering Vouilly, look for a Chambres d'Hôtes sign directing you to turn right onto a winding road—follow it to the Hamels' driveway.

LE CHÂTEAU (Gîtes de France)
Hosts: Marie-Jose & James Hamel
Vouilly, 14230 Isigny-sur-Mer, France
Tel: 02.31.22.08.59, Fax: 02.31.22.90.58
www.karenbrown.com/france/lechateau.html
5 rooms, 1 with private bathroom
Double: 300F–330F
No table d'hôte; Ferme Auberge nearby
Open Mar to Dec, Very little English spoken
Credit cards: MC, VS
Region: Normandy; Michelin Map 231

Nestled on the shore of Lake Geneva, the tiny walled medieval village of Yvoire is positively captivating—almost too quaint to be real. Her allure is even more captivating in summer when every available bit of land is a flower garden and every house draped with red geraniums. Making everything perfect, there is a gem of a small hotel here—the 200-year-old Hôtel du Port which absolutely oozes charm with a stone façade almost totally covered with ivy, brown shutters, and red geraniums spilling out of windowboxes. It is just next to the dock where ferries flit in and out all day, making their circuit around the lake. The main focus of the hotel is its restaurant which has a summer dining terrace stretching to the edge of the water. Although the majority of guests come just for lunch, for a lucky few there are four sweet bedrooms available. If you want to splurge, request one of the two in front with a romantic balcony overlooking the lake. The moderately sized, spotlessly clean guestrooms are simple and attractive, with built-in wooden furniture and matching drapes and bedspreads. Each has a modern bathroom, air conditioning, telephone, TV, and mini-bar. As in so many of our favorite hotels, the gracious owners, Jeannine & Jean-François Kung, are also the managers, always keeping an eye out to be sure the hotel is impeccable in every way. *Directions:* Yvoire is on the south shore of Lake Geneva, 30 km east of Geneva.

HÔTEL DU PORT
Hosts: Jeannine & Jean-François Kung
74104 Yvoire, France
Tel: 04.50.72.80.17, Fax: 04.50.72.90.71
4 rooms
Double: 550F–800F
Open mid-Mar to Nov, Very good English spoken
Credit cards: all major
No table d'hôte; restaurant
Region: Haute-Savoie; Michelin Map 244

Key and Regional Map

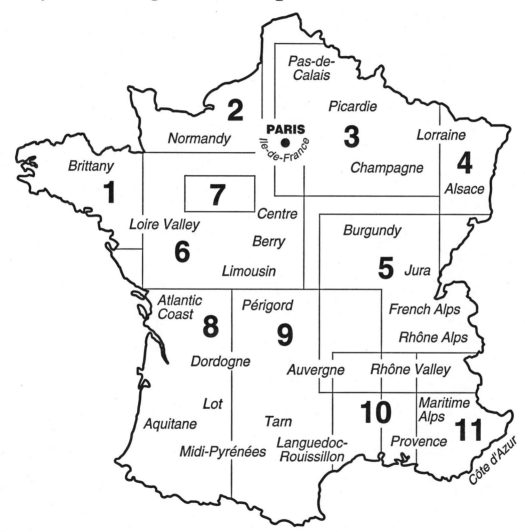

- **Brittany** — 1
- **Normandy** — 2
- Pas-de-Calais
- Picardie
- **PARIS** Ile-de-France
- Lorraine
- **3**
- **4**
- Champagne
- Alsace
- **7**
- Loire Valley
- Centre
- **6**
- Berry
- Burgundy
- **5** Jura
- Limousin
- Atlantic Coast
- Périgord
- **8**
- **9**
- French Alps
- Rhône Alps
- Dordogne
- Auvergne
- Rhône Valley
- Lot
- **10**
- Maritime Alps
- Aquitane
- Tarn
- Languedoc-Rouissillon
- Provence
- **11**
- Midi-Pyrénées
- Côte d'Azur

Map 1

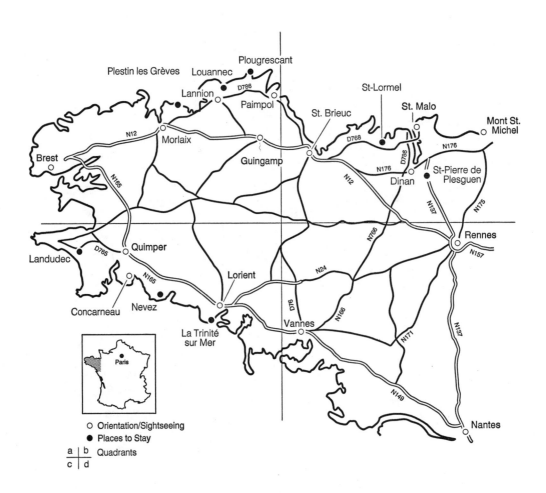

Plougrescant

Plestin les Grèves   Louannec

Lannion   D786

St-Lormel

Paimpol   St. Malo

St. Brieuc   Mont St.
Michel

Morlaix   D768

Brest   Guingamp   St-Pierre de
Plesguen

N12   N176

N165   N12   Dinan

N766   N176   D786

N137   N175

Rennes

N157

Quimper   N24

Landudec   D765

N165   Lorient   D76

Nevez   N166

Concarneau   Vannes

La Trinité   N171   N137
sur Mer

N149

Nantes

Paris

○ Orientation/Sightseeing
● Places to Stay

a	b
c	d

Quadrants

196

Map 2

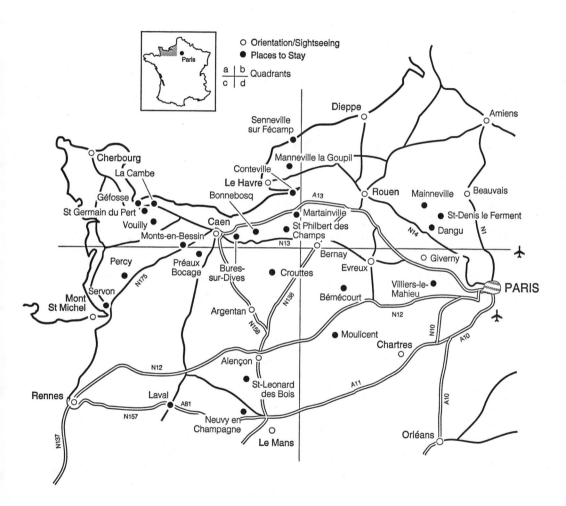

Orientation/Sightseeing ○
Places to Stay ●

a | b
c | d Quadrants

Paris

Dieppe
Amiens
Senneville sur Fécamp
Manneville la Goupil
Conteville
Le Havre
Bonnebosq
Cherbourg
La Cambe
Géfosse
St Germain du Pert
Vouilly
Monts-en-Bessin
Caen
Martainville
St Philbert des Champs
Rouen
Mainneville
Beauvais
St-Denis le Ferment
Dangu
A13
N14
N1
Percy
Préaux Bocage
Bures-sur-Dives
Croutes
Bernay
Evreux
Giverny
PARIS
Mont St Michel
Servon
Argentan
Bémécourt
Villiers-le-Mahieu
Moulicent
Chartres
N175
N158
N138
N13
N12
N10
A10
Rennes
N12
Laval
A81
Alençon
St-Leonard des Bois
A11
Orléans
N137
N157
Neuvy en Champagne
Le Mans
A10

197

Map 3

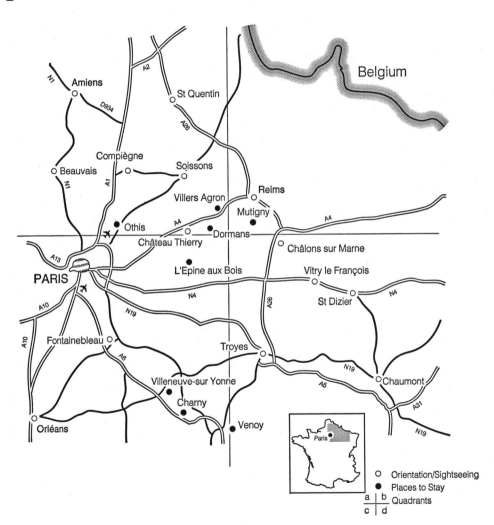

Map 4

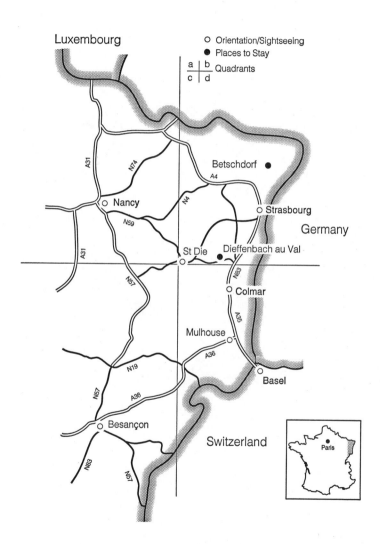

Luxembourg

○ Orientation/Sightseeing
● Places to Stay

a	b
c	d	Quadrants

A31

N74

Betschdorf ●

A4

○ Nancy

N4

N59

○ Strasbourg

Germany

A31

St Die ○ Dieffenbach au Val ●

N57

N83

○ Colmar

A35

Mulhouse ○

A36

N19

○ Basel

N57

A36

○ Besançon

Switzerland

N83

N57

Paris

Map 5

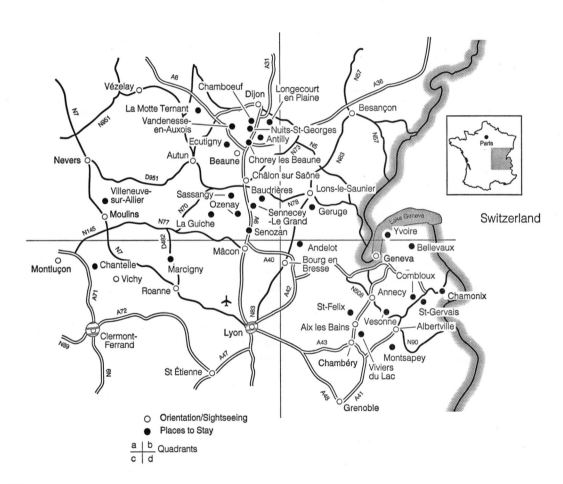

Vézelay

Chamboeuf   Dijon   Longecourt
en Plaine

A6   Besançon

La Motte Ternant   N57   A36

Vandenesse-
en-Auxois   Nuits-St-Georges

Ecutigny   Antilly   N5   N57

Autun   Beaune   Chorey les Beaune   N83

Nevers   Châlon sur Saône

D951   Baudrières   Lons-le-Saunier

Villeneuve-
sur-Allier   Sassangy   N78   Lake Geneva

Moulins   Ozenay   N70   Sennecey   Geruge

N145   La Guiche   Senozan   Yvoire

N77   A6   Bellevaux

Mâcon   Andelot   Geneva

Montluçon   Chantelle   D482   A40   Bourg en   Combloux
Bresse

Vichy   Marcigny   N505   Annecy   Chamonix

A71   Roanne   A42   St-Felix   St-Gervais

A72   N83   Aix les Bains   Vesonne   Albertville

N89   Clermont-
Ferrand   Lyon   A43   Chambéry   Montsapey   N90

N2   St Étienne   A47   Viviers
du Lac

A48   A41

Grenoble

Switzerland

Paris

○ Orientation/Sightseeing

● Places to Stay

a | b
c | d   Quadrants

200

Map 6

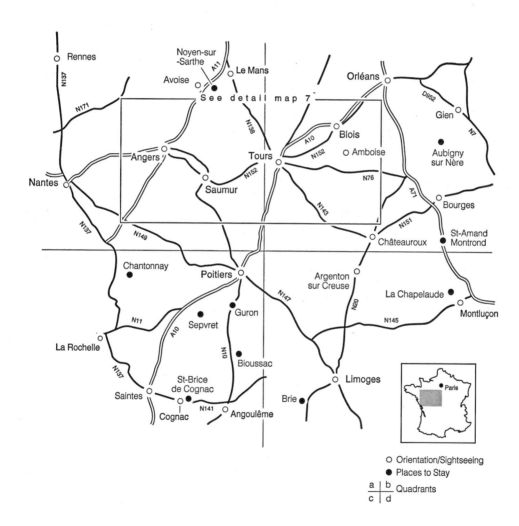

Rennes

Noyen-sur-Sarthe

Avoise

Le Mans

Orléans

See detail map 7

Gien

Blois

Angers

Amboise

Aubigny sur Nère

Tours

Nantes

Saumur

Bourges

St-Amand Montrond

Chantonnay

Châteauroux

Poitiers

Argenton sur Creuse

La Chapelaude

Guron

Montluçon

Sepvret

La Rochelle

Bioussac

St-Brice de Cognac

Limoges

Saintes

Brie

Cognac

Angoulême

Paris

○ Orientation/Sightseeing
● Places to Stay

a	b
c	d

Quadrants

Map 7

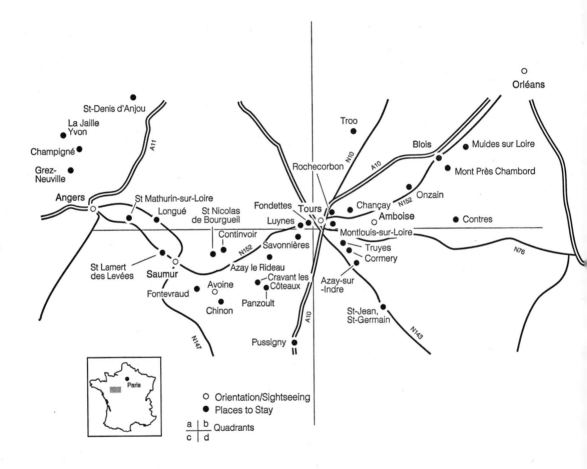

St-Denis d'Anjou
La Jaille Yvon
Champigné
Grez-Neuville
Angers
St Mathurin-sur-Loire
Longué
St Nicolas de Bourgueil
St Lamert des Levées
Saumur
Fontevraud
Avoine
Chinon
Continvoir
Azay le Rideau
Cravant les Côteaux
Panzoult
Pussigny
Fondettes
Luynes
Savonnières
Tours
Rochecorbon
Troo
Chançay
Amboise
Montlouis-sur-Loire
Truyes
Cormery
Azay-sur-Indre
St-Jean, St-Germain
Blois
Onzain
Muides sur Loire
Mont Près Chambord
Contres
Orléans

A11
N10
A10
N152
A10
N147
N143
N76

Paris

○ Orientation/Sightseeing
● Places to Stay

a	b
c	d

Quadrants

Map 8

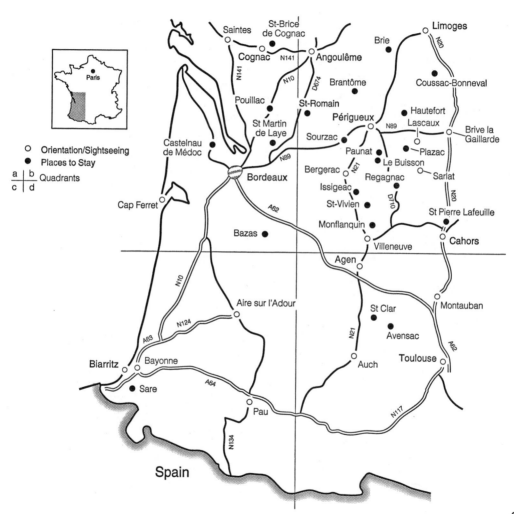

Orientation/Sightseeing
○ Places to Stay
●

a	b
c	d	Quadrants

Saintes
St-Brice de Cognac
Brie
Limoges
Cognac N141 Angoulême
Coussac-Bonneval
Brantôme
Pouillac
St-Romain
St Martin de Laye
Périgueux
Hautefort
Lascaux
Castelnau de Médoc
Sourzac
Brive la Gaillarde
Paunat
Plazac
Bergerac
Le Buisson
Bordeaux
Regagnac
Sarlat
Issigeac
Cap Ferret
St-Vivien
St Pierre Lafeuille
Monflanquin
Bazas
Villeneuve
Cahors
Agen
Montauban
Aire sur l'Adour
St Clar
Avensac
Biarritz Bayonne
Toulouse
Auch
Sare
Pau
Spain

Map 9

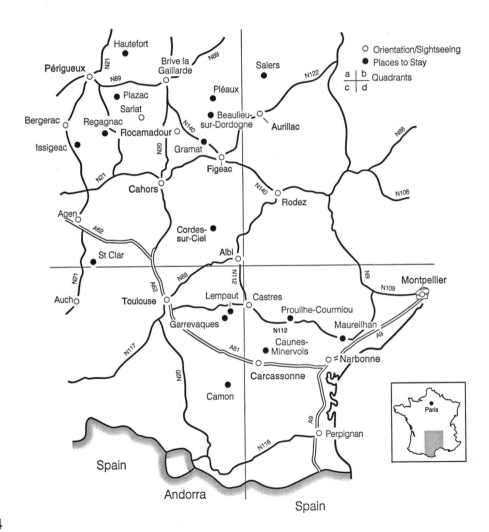

Hautefort

Périgueux

N21

N89

N89

Brive la
Gaillarde

N89

Salers

N122

Plazac

Pléaux

Sarlat

Beaulieu-
sur-Dordogne

Bergerac

Regagnac

N140

Aurillac

Rocamadour

N88

Issigeac

Gramat

N20

N21

Figeac

Cahors

N140

Rodez

N106

Agen

A62

Cordes-
sur-Ciel

Albi

St Clar

N21

A62

N88

N112

N9

Montpellier

N109

Auch

Toulouse

Lempaut

Castres

Prouilhe-Courmiou

Garrevaques

Maureilhan

N112

A9

N117

A61

Caunes-
Minervois

A62

Narbonne

Carcassonne

N20

Camon

A9

Perpignan

N116

Spain

Andorra

Spain

○ Orientation/Sightseeing
● Places to Stay

a	b
c	d

Quadrants

Paris

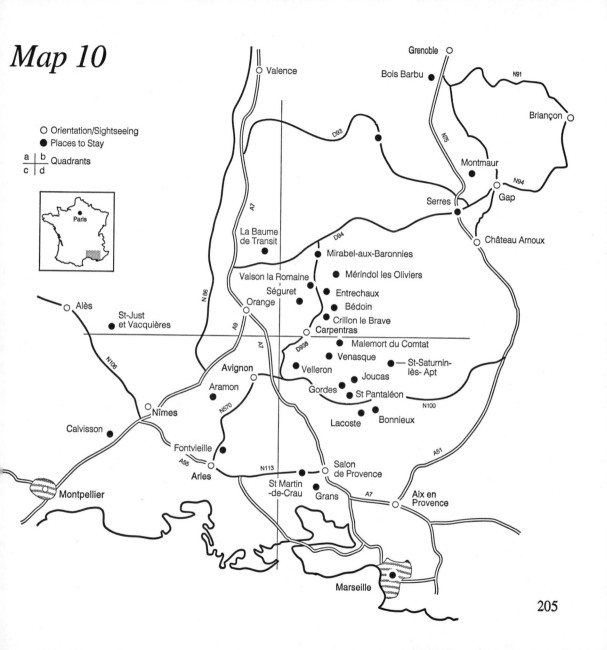

Map 10

○ Orientation/Sightseeing
● Places to Stay

a	b
c	d

Quadrants

Paris

Grenoble
Bois Barbu
Briançon
N91
Valence
D93
Montmaur
N75
N94
Serres
Gap
Château Arnoux
A7
La Baume
de Transit
D94
Mirabel-aux-Baronnies
Mérindol les Oliviers
N 86
Vaison la Romaine
Séguret
Entrechaux
Alès
Orange
Bédoin
St-Just
et Vacquières
A9
Crillon le Brave
Carpentras
A7
Malemort du Comtat
D938
Venasque
St-Saturnin-
lès- Apt
N106
Avignon
Velleron
Joucas
Aramon
Gordes
St Pantaléon
N100
Nîmes
N570
Lacoste
Bonnieux
Calvisson
Fontvieille
A55
Arles
N113
Salon
de Provence
St Martin
-de-Crau
A51
Grans
A7
Aix en
Provence
Montpellier
Marseille

Map 11

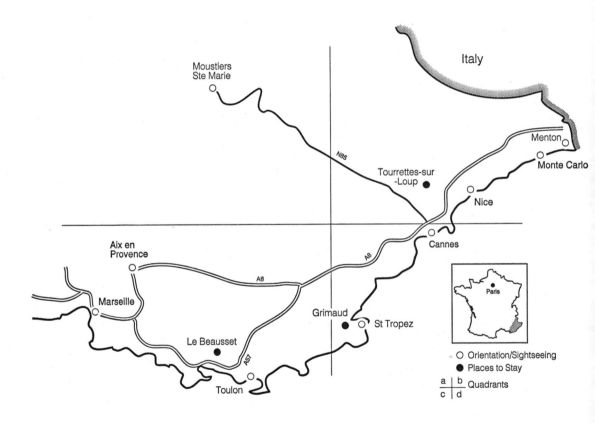

Moustiers
Ste Marie

Italy

N85

Menton

Monte Carlo

Tourrettes-sur
-Loup

Nice

Cannes

Aix en
Provence

A8

A8

Marseille

Paris

Grimaud

St Tropez

Le Beausset

A57

Toulon

○ Orientation/Sightseeing
● Places to Stay

a	b
c	d

Quadrants

Index

P

Panzoult
   Domaine de Beauséjour, 128
Pastourelle (La), Saint Lormel, 154
Patrus (Les), L'Épine aux Bois, 73
Paunat
   Le Moulin Neuf, 129
Percy
   Le Moulin Girard, 130
Petit Pey (Le), Issigeac, 90
Petit Simone, La Chapelaude, 53
Pets, 9
Plaisance, Othis-Beaumarchais, 126
Plazac
   Les Tilleuls, 131
Pléaux-Ally
   Château de La Vigne, 132
Plestin Les Grèves
   Ty Pesketer, 133
Plougrescant
   Manoir de Kergrec'h, 134
Poiriers Roses (La Ferme des), Saint Philbert des Champs, 160
Portal (Chez), Le Viviers du Lac, 193
Port-Guyet (Manoir du), Saint Nicolas de Bourgueil, 158
Pouillac-La Galèz
   La Thébaïde, 135
Préaux Bocage
   La Crête aux Oiseaux, 136
Pressoir (La Ferme du), Conteville, 59
Prouilhe-Courniou
   La Métairie Basse, 137
Prudent (Chez), Salers, 166

Pussigny
   Le Clos Saint-Clair, 138

Q

Quart (Le), Luynes, 100

R

Rabouillère (La), Contres, 61
Rates, 9
Regagnac
   Château de Regagnac, 139
Reservations
   Cancellations, 12
   Check In, 11
   Deposits, 10
   General Information, 10
   Making Reservations by Fax, 11
   Making Reservations by Mail, 11
   Making Reservations by Telephone, 11
   Reservation Letter in French and English, 14
Rochecorbon
   Château de Montgouverne, 140
Rocher Point (Le), Aramon, 18
Roussillon (Château de), Saint Pierre Lafeuille, 162
Rouvre (Le Petit Moulin du), Saint Pierre de Pleguen, 161

S

Saint Amand-Montrond
   Château de La Commanderie, 141
Saint Brice de Cognac
   Les Vollauds, 142
Saint Clar
   Chez Cournot, 143

SHARE YOUR REVIEWS WITH US

We greatly appreciate first-hand evaluations of places in our guides. Your critiques are invaluable to us. To keep current on the properties in our guides, we keep a database of readers' comments.

Please list your comments about properties you have visited. We welcome accolades, as well as criticisms.

Name of hotel or b&b _____ Town _____ Country _____

Comments:

Name of hotel or b&b _____ Town _____ Country _____

Comments:

Your name _____ Street _____ Town _____ State _____

Zip _____ Country _____ Tel _____ e-mail _____ date _____

Please send report to: Karen Brown's Guides, Post Office Box 70, San Mateo, California 94401, USA
tel: (650) 342-9117, fax: (650) 342-9153, e-mail: karen@karenbrown.com, www.karenbrown.com

SHARE YOUR REVIEWS WITH US

We greatly appreciate first-hand evaluations of places in our guides. Your critiques are invaluable to us. To keep current on the properties in our guides, we keep a database of readers' comments.

Please list your comments about properties you have visited. We welcome accolades, as well as criticisms.

Name of hotel or b&b _____ Town _____ Country _____
Comments:

Name of hotel or b&b _____ Town _____ Country _____
Comments:

Your name _____ Street _____ Town _____ State _____
Zip _____ Country _____ Tel _____ e-mail _____ date _____

Please send report to: Karen Brown's Guides, Post Office Box 70, San Mateo, California 94401, USA
tel: (650) 342-9117, fax: (650) 342-9153, e-mail: karen@karenbrown.com, www.karenbrown.com

SHARE YOUR REVIEWS WITH US

We greatly appreciate first-hand evaluations of places in our guides. Your critiques are invaluable to us. To keep current on the properties in our guides, we keep a database of readers' comments.

Please list your comments about properties you have visited. We welcome accolades, as well as criticisms.

Name of hotel or b&b _____ Town _____ Country _____

Comments:

Name of hotel or b&b _____ Town _____ Country _____

Comments:

Your name _____ Street _____ Town _____ State _____

Zip _____ Country _____ Tel _____ e-mail _____ date _____

Please send report to: Karen Brown's Guides, Post Office Box 70, San Mateo, California 94401, USA
tel: (650) 342-9117, fax: (650) 342-9153, e-mail: karen@karenbrown.com, www.karenbrown.com

SHARE YOUR REVIEWS WITH US

We greatly appreciate first-hand evaluations of places in our guides. Your critiques are invaluable to us. To keep current on the properties in our guides, we keep a database of readers' comments.

Please list your comments about properties you have visited. We welcome accolades, as well as criticisms.

Name of hotel or b&b _____ Town _____ Country _____
Comments:

Name of hotel or b&b _____ Town _____ Country _____
Comments:

Your name _____ Street _____ Town _____ State _____
Zip _____ Country _____ Tel _____ e-mail _____ date _____

Please send report to: Karen Brown's Guides, Post Office Box 70, San Mateo, California 94401, USA
tel: (650) 342-9117, fax: (650) 342-9153, e-mail: karen@karenbrown.com, www.karenbrown.com

SHARE YOUR DISCOVERIES WITH US

Outstanding properties often come from readers' discoveries. We would love to hear from you.

Please list below any hotel or bed & breakfast you discover. Tell us what you liked about the property and, if possible, please include a brochure or photographs so we can share your enthusiasm. We keep a permanent database of all of your recommendations for future use. Note: we regret we cannot return photos.

Owner _____ Hotel or B&B _____ Street _____

Town _____ Zip _____ State or Region _____ Country _____

Comments:

Your name _____ Street _____ Town _____ State _____

Zip _____ Country _____ Tel _____ e-mail _____ date _____

Please send report to: Karen Brown's Guides, Post Office Box 70, San Mateo, California 94401, USA
tel: (650) 342-9117, fax: (650) 342-9153, e-mail: karen@karenbrown.com, www.karenbrown.com

SHARE YOUR DISCOVERIES WITH US

Outstanding properties often come from readers' discoveries. We would love to hear from you.

Please list below any hotel or bed & breakfast you discover. Tell us what you liked about the property and, if possible, please include a brochure or photographs so we can share your enthusiasm. We keep a permanent database of all of your recommendations for future use. Note: we regret we cannot return photos.

Owner _____ Hotel or B&B _____ Street _____

Town _____ Zip _____ State or Region _____ Country _____

Comments:

Your name _____ Street _____ Town _____ State _____

Zip _____ Country _____ Tel _____ e-mail _____ date _____

Please send report to: Karen Brown's Guides, Post Office Box 70, San Mateo, California 94401, USA
tel: (650) 342-9117, fax: (650) 342-9153, e-mail: karen@karenbrown.com, www.karenbrown.com

SHARE YOUR DISCOVERIES WITH US

Outstanding properties often come from readers' discoveries. We would love to hear from you.

Please list below any hotel or bed & breakfast you discover. Tell us what you liked about the property and, if possible, please include a brochure or photographs so we can share your enthusiasm. We keep a permanent database of all of your recommendations for future use. Note: we regret we cannot return photos.

Owner _____ Hotel or B&B _____ Street _____

Town _____ Zip _____ State or Region _____ Country _____

Comments:

Your name _____ Street _____ Town _____ State _____

Zip _____ Country _____ Tel _____ e-mail _____ date _____

Please send report to: Karen Brown's Guides, Post Office Box 70, San Mateo, California 94401, USA
tel: (650) 342-9117, fax: (650) 342-9153, e-mail: karen@karenbrown.com, www.karenbrown.com

SHARE YOUR DISCOVERIES WITH US

Outstanding properties often come from readers' discoveries. We would love to hear from you.

Please list below any hotel or bed & breakfast you discover. Tell us what you liked about the property and, if possible, please include a brochure or photographs so we can share your enthusiasm. We keep a permanent database of all of your recommendations for future use. Note: we regret we cannot return photos.

Owner _____ Hotel or B&B _____ Street _____

Town _____ Zip _____ State or Region _____ Country _____

Comments:

Your name _____ Street _____ Town _____ State _____

Zip _____ Country _____ Tel _____ e-mail _____ date _____

Please send report to: Karen Brown's Guides, Post Office Box 70, San Mateo, California 94401, USA
tel: (650) 342-9117, fax: (650) 342-9153, e-mail: karen@karenbrown.com, www.karenbrown.com

KB Travel Service

Quality * Personal Service * Great Values

- Staff trained by Karen Brown to help you plan your holiday
- Special offerings on airfares to major cities in Europe
- Special prices on car rentals with free upgrades
- Countryside mini-itineraries based on Karen Brown's Guides
- Reservations for hotels, inns, and B&Bs in Karen Brown's Guides

For assistance and information on service fees contact:

KB Travel Service
16 East Third Avenue
San Mateo, California, 94401, USA
tel: 800-782-2128, fax: 650-342-2519, email: kbtravel@aol.com

---

For additional information on places in the Karen Brown's Guides, visit the following websites:
www.karenbrown.com and www.innsandouts.com

✈ UNITED AIRLINES

is the

Preferred Airline

of

Karen Brown's Guides

and

Karen Brown Travel Services

Seal Cove Inn

Located in the San Francisco Bay Area

Karen Brown Herbert (best known as author of the Karen Brown's guides) and her husband, Rick, have put 20 years of experience into reality and opened their own superb hideaway, Seal Cove Inn. Spectacularly set amongst wild flowers and bordered by towering cypress trees, Seal Cove Inn looks out to the distant ocean over acres of county park: an oasis where you can enjoy secluded beaches, explore tidepools, watch frolicking seals, and follow the tree-lined path that traces the windswept ocean bluffs. Country antiques, original watercolors, flower-laden cradles, rich fabrics, and the gentle ticking of grandfather clocks create the perfect ambiance for a foggy day in front of the crackling log fire. Each bedroom is its own haven with a cozy sitting area before a wood-burning fireplace and doors opening onto a private balcony or patio with views to the park and ocean. Moss Beach is a 35-minute drive south of San Francisco, 6 miles north of the picturesque town of Half Moon Bay, and a few minutes from Princeton harbor with its colorful fishing boats and restaurants. Seal Cove Inn makes a perfect base for whale-watching, salmon-fishing excursions, day trips to San Francisco, exploring the coast, or, best of all, just a romantic interlude by the sea, time to relax and be pampered. Karen and Rick look forward to the pleasure of welcoming you to their coastal hideaway.

Seal Cove Inn • 221 Cypress Avenue • Moss Beach • California • 94038 • USA
tel: (650) 728-4114, fax: (650) 728-4116, e-mail: sealcove@coastside.net, website: sealcoveinn.com

CLARE BROWN has many years of experience in the field of travel and has earned the designation of Certified Travel Consultant. Since 1969 she has specialized in planning itineraries to Europe using charming small hotels in the countryside for her clients. The focus of her job remains unchanged, but now her expertise is available to a larger audience—the readers of her daughter's country inn guides. Clare lives in Hillsborough, California, with her husband, Bill.

BARBARA TAPP, the talented artist who produces all of the hotel sketches and delightful illustrations in this guide, was raised in Australia where she studied in Sydney at the School of Interior Design. Although Barbara continues with freelance projects, she devotes much of her time to illustrating the Karen Brown guides. Barbara lives in Kensington, California, with her husband, Richard, their two sons, Jonothan and Alexander, and daughter, Georgia.

JANN POLLARD, the artist responsible for the beautiful painting on the cover of this guide, has studied art since childhood, and is well-known for her outstanding impressionistic-style watercolors which she has exhibited in numerous juried shows, winning many awards. Jann travels frequently to Europe (using Karen Brown's guides) where she loves to paint historical buildings. Jann lives in Burlingame, California, with her husband, Gene.

Travel Your Dreams • Order your Karen Brown Guides Today

Please ask in your local bookstore for Karen Brown's Guides. If the books you want are unavailable, you may order directly from the publisher. Books will be shipped immediately.

_____ *Austria: Charming Inns & Itineraries* $17.95

_____ *California: Charming Inns & Itineraries* $17.95

_____ *England: Charming Bed & Breakfasts* $16.95

_____ *England, Wales & Scotland: Charming Hotels & Itineraries* $17.95

_____ *France: Charming Bed & Breakfasts* $16.95

_____ *France: Charming Inns & Itineraries* $17.95

_____ *Germany: Charming Inns & Itineraries* $17.95

_____ *Ireland: Charming Inns & Itineraries* $17.95

_____ *Italy: Charming Bed & Breakfasts* $16.95

_____ *Italy: Charming Inns & Itineraries* $17.95

_____ *Portugal: Charming Inns & Itineraries* $17.95

_____ *Spain: Charming Inns & Itineraries* $17.95

_____ *Switzerland: Charming Inns & Itineraries* $17.95

Name _____ Street _____

Town _____ State _____ Zip _____ Tel _____ email _____

Credit Card (MasterCard or Visa) _____ Expires: _____

For orders in the USA, add $4 for the first book and $1 for each additional book for shipment. California residents add 8.25% sales tax. Overseas orders add $10 per book for airmail shipment. Indicate number of copies of each title; fax or mail form with check or credit card information to:

KAREN BROWN'S GUIDES
Post Office Box 70 • San Mateo • California • 94401 • USA
tel: (650) 342-9117, fax: (650) 342-9153, e-mail: karen@karenbrown.com

For additional information about Karen Brown's Guides, visit our website at www.karenbrown.com